Download Audio

音声ファイル
無料 DL
のご案内

このテキストの音声を無料で視聴（ストリーミング）・ダウンロードできます。自習用音声としてご活用ください。
以下のサイトにアクセスしてテキスト番号で検索してください。

https://nanun-do.com　テキスト番号［ **512098** ］

※ 無線 LAN（WiFi）に接続してのご利用を推奨いたします。

※ 音声ダウンロードは Zip ファイルでの提供になります。
お使いの機器によっては別途ソフトウェア（アプリケーション）の導入が必要となります。

※ Companion to TOEIC Bridge L&R Tests 音声ダウンローページは以下の QR コードからもご利用になれます。

Read by

Chris Koprowski（米）
Guy Perryman（英）
Shizuka Anderson（加）
Sarah Greaves（豪）

Companion to TOEIC Bridge® L&R Tests

大学生のためのTOEIC Bridge® L&R Tests演習

Esther WAER
UCHIDA Masakatsu
KAMEYAMA Hiroyuki

NAN'UN-DO

FOREWORD by the authors

For many students a TOEIC score is an important marker of their progress in English. It can also be a good way to get motivated to study, and is often needed for applications for new positions or promotions. These are all valid reasons to work hard. English is a skill in high demand, especially as the business world is growing ever closer with the increased use of internet meetings and online business. People from all over the world now need to communicate, not only for transactions, but also to build effective working relationships. It is clear that one must not only be able to use and understand English but also be able to communicate ideas, thoughts, and feelings effectively.

As the saying goes, practice makes perfect, and practice is exactly what this textbook intends to provide. A multitude of opportunities to practice for the TOEIC Bridge test. This book consists of practical TOEIC Bridge exercises and provides a great variety of TOEIC-style questions. Each chapter focuses on a different theme and grammar point. The topics are highly relevant to young adults and should be applicable beyond the test in a daily communicative context. This textbook offers you an effective way to study whether or not you are taking the test.

Each chapter is divided equally between listening and reading. The listening section starts with a short exercise focusing on vocabulary and Part1, the picture section. Building up to Part 2, where you will hear questions and be asked to choose the correct response. Next comes Part 3, with questions about short conversations and finally you will answer questions about a variety of talks. The reading section consists of sentence completion exercises, followed by questions for completing texts, and then finally reading comprehension practice. There are tips on test strategies scattered throughout the book to help you achieve your goals.

Enjoyable topics which are relevant to daily life should make it easier to work through the book to the end. As we all know continuation is the key to success in any field. This textbook can be used alone, or even better when used in combination with Companion to English Communication which focuses on reading and speaking. You can be assured of covering all your bases on your quest to fluency in English.

Table of Contents

<Stage 1>

<Stage 2>

Stage 1

Unit 1 Friends

Grammar Target: Present tense

Vocabulary Check

02

Listen to the following sentences and fill in the blanks.

(a) I'm (   ) I (   ) a (   ).

(b) The (   ) are very (   ).

(c) It (   ) (   ) a lot of (   ).

(d) (   ) (   ) to coffee.

(e) Please (   ) your room (   ).

(f) We (   ) about (   ).

Listening Section Practice

Part 1 03

[1] Choose the picture that the phrase or sentence best describes.

(A)

(B)

(C)

(D)

[2] Listen again to the sentence and fill in the blanks.

A boy (   ) (   ) (   ).

Strategies for TOEIC BRIDGE #1

Listening Part 1 – Four Pictures

In this section you will hear a sentence or phrase. You will then be asked to choose one picture from four that best matches the sentence or phrase.

Try to determine if the sentence or phrase is about one or more people, and whether they are male or female. When you hear a sentence without people try to identify what is happening.

Part 2 04

[1] Listen to questions or statements. After each question or statement, you will hear and read four responses. Choose the best response.

(1) (A) Yes, I am. (B) Yes, you are.
(C) How about it? (D) Good, and you?

(2) (A) Yes, I am. (B) Yes, I do.
(C) Who are they? (D) Is he?

(3) (A) They are out. (B) I'm in the office.
(C) Teachers do. (D) On the second floor.

(4) (A) Yes, I love it. (B) No, I don't.
(C) I like science fiction. (D) The class is over.

(5) (A) Let's turn on the heating. (B) Clean the room.
(C) Yes, it is. (D) No, I don't.

[2] Listen again to each question or statement and fill in the blanks.

(1) Hi, (   ) (   ) (   )?
(2) (   ) (   ) (   ) Mr. Walsh?
(3) (   ) (   ) the teachers' (   )?
(4) (   ) (   ) (   ) the science class?
(5) (   ) (   ) in this room.

Part 3 05

Listen to some short conversations. You will hear and read two questions about each conversation. Choose the best answer to each question.

[1] Questions (1) and (2) refer to the following conversation.

(1) How does the man look?
(A) Happy. (B) Sad. (C) Angry. (D) Sick.

(2) What does the woman suggest the man do?
(A) Go to work. (B) See his family. (C) Go to a clinic. (D) Have a fever.

[2] Questions (3) and (4) refer to the following conversation.

(3) How does the woman look?
(A) Great. (B) Strange. (C) Tired. (D) Sad.

(4) What does the woman say about the gym?
(A) The lesson is boring. (B) The instructor is wonderful.
(C) The room is messy. (D) The floor is slippery.

Part 4 06

Listen to some short talks. You will hear and read two questions about each talk. Choose the best answer to each question.

[1] Questions (1) and (2) refer to the following talk.

(1) What day is it?
(A) Sunday.
(B) Monday.
(C) Tuesday.
(D) Friday.

(2) What will they talk about?
(A) Politics.
(B) Tea.
(C) Religion.
(D) Art.

[2] Questions (3) and (4) refer to the following phone message.

(3) What will Jane take to the party?
(A) Wine.
(B) Paintings.
(C) Snacks.
(D) Plates.

(4) What time will Jane go to the party?
(A) At 3.
(B) At 5.
(C) At 7.
(D) At 10.

Reading Section Practice

Part 1

Each sentence has a space where a word or phrase is missing. Choose the best answer to complete the sentence.

(1) _________ you a member of this gym?
(A) Do (B) Is (C) Are (D) Can

(2) She _________ speak French but she speaks Spanish.
(A) isn't (B) aren't (C) don't (D) doesn't

(3) _________ he belong to the tennis club?
(A) Is (B) Are (C) Do (D) Does

(4) One of our cats _________ outside walking now.
(A) is (B) are (C) do (D) does

(5) Please _________ off the grass.
(A) have (B) do (C) keep (D) say

(6) There _________ a few nice restaurants in this area.
(A) is (B) are (C) has (D) does

(7) Heather _________ her son to Spain last year.
(A) take (B) takes (C) took (D) taking

(8) I _________ a stranger here myself.
(A) am (B) like (C) come (D) make

Part 2

Each of the short texts has three spaces where a word or phrase is missing. For each space, choose the best answer to complete the text.

[1] Questions (1) to (3) refer to the following memo.

Hi Ruth,

I am going to see the movie. Tom Henley [(1)] in it. I love him.
[(2)] you have free time on Sunday? If you [(3)] to join me, please call me.

Greg

(1) (A) is	(B) are	(C) play	(D) do
(2) (A) Is	(B) Are	(C) Do	(D) Have
(3) (A) watch	(B) break	(C) thank	(D) want

[2] Questions (4) to (6) refer to the following notice.

POTLUCK PARTY

Welcome to Horace Green College!

How [(4)] your new school life going?

Please [(5)] some food and join the party.

It's a great opportunity to make new friends!

All students [(6)] welcome.

Place: The 1st floor Lounge Room

Time: September 29. 18:00 - 20:00

(4) (A) is	(B) are	(C) do	(D) does
(5) (A) come	(B) lend	(C) sell	(D) bring
(6) (A) is	(B) are	(C) invite	(D) create

Part 3

Texts such as notices, letters and instant messages are followed by two or three questions. Choose the best answer to each question.

[1] Questions (1) and (2) refer to the following advertisement.

Jazz Night

Blue Rooms - 21st Friday June

Live Performances

7:30 P.M. Stevie Bland on Saxophone with the Ragtime Trio.
8:15 P.M. Evie Findley - with James Trelis on piano
9:30 P.M until late – open jam session

Tickets $15 on the door, $10 in advance.
Tickets can be purchased online or in JB Records.

(1) What will happen on June 21?
(A) A record signing
(B) A music lesson
(C) A jazz competition
(D) A music event

(2) Where can people buy a cheap ticket?
(A) At the club
(B) On the internet
(C) From Stevie Bland
(D) At a jam session

[2] Questions (3) and (4) refer to the following text message.

Lisa: I haven't seen you for a long time! How are you? I was busy with my exams, but I'm finished now. - I think I passed them. - Do you want to go out this weekend?

Michelle: Hi. Yes, it has been a long time!
Sorry, but I already have plans this weekend.

Lisa: That's too bad.

Michelle: ______________________________

(3) What does Lisa do?
(A) She is a teacher.
(B) She is a student.
(C) She likes to study.
(D) She finished her test.

(4) Select the best sentence for Michelle's message.
(A) "How about next weekend?"
(B) "So I can meet you on Saturday."
(C) "How about that new restaurant?"
(D) "Sure, let's meet on Sunday."

Unit 2 Hobbies

Grammar Target:
Infinitive and Gerund, Adverbs of Frequency

Vocabulary Check 07

Listen to the following sentences and fill in the blanks.

(a) Nancy (　　　　　) (　　　　　) (　　　　　).

(b) My hobbies (　　　　　) (　　　　　).

(c) I take a piano lesson (　　　　　) (　　　　　) (　　　　　).

(d) George (　　　　　) (　　　　　) Mont Blanc (　　　　　).

(e) Yoko (　　　　　) (　　　　　) (　　　　　) in Chinese.

(f) The text for this class is (　　　　　) (　　　　　).

Listening Section Practice

Part 1 08

[1] Choose the picture that the phrase or sentence best describes.

(A)

(B)

(C)

(D)

[2] Listen again to the sentence and fill in the blanks.

A woman (　　　　　) a (　　　　　) (　　　　　).

Part 2 09

[1] Listen to questions or statements. After each question or statement, you will hear and read four responses. Choose the best response.

(1) (A) I do. (B) Tomorrow.
(C) Every other day. (D) John does.

(2) (A) Yes, I'm a cook. (B) To eat dinner.
(C) Let's have lunch. (D) Yes, her dishes are great.

(3) (A) It's on fire. (B) Yes, I am.
(C) Please stop it. (D) It's good for him.

(4) (A) It smells good. (B) Yes, after each meal.
(C) Regular size. (D) Yes, it's allowed.

(5) (A) I'm on top of it. (B) Very high.
(C) Only once. (D) You have.

[2] Listen again to each question or statement and fill in the blanks.

(1) John, (   ) (   ) do you go for a (   )?
(2) Susan (   ) (   ), (   ) she?
(3) Paul (   ) (   ) (   ).
(4) Do you (   ) (   ) (   )?
(5) (   ) (   ) (   ) have you (   ) Mt. Fuji?

Part 3 10

Listen to some short conversations. You will hear and read two questions about each conversation. Choose the best answer to each question.

[1] Questions (1) and (2) refer to the following conversation.

(1) Who is Mr. McInotosh?
(A) A runner. (B) A studio musician.
(C) A postman. (D) A dance instructor.

(2) What will the woman probably do?
(A) Take a lesson. (B) Give a lecture.
(C) Practice running. (D) Stay at home.

[2] Questions (3) and (4) refer to the following conversation.

(3) What day does the man NOT go to the gym?
(A) Everyday. (B) On Saturday. (C) On Sunday. (D) Every other day.

(4) What does the woman like to do on weekends?
(A) Swim at the beach. (B) Go cycling.
(C) See her bike. (D) Ride a motorcycle.

Where there's a will, there's a way. [proverb]

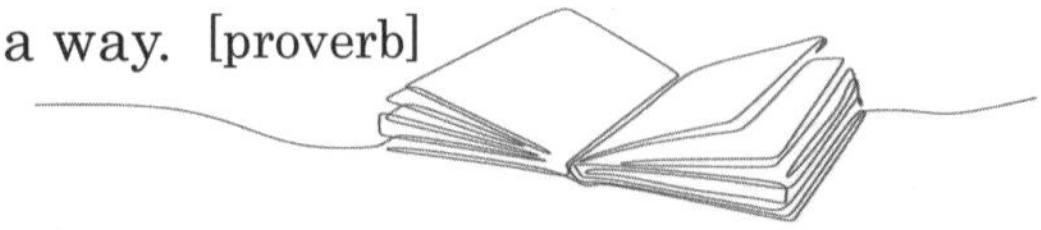

Part 4 11

Listen to some short talks. You will hear and read two questions about each talk. Choose the best answer to each question.

[1] Questions (1) and (2) refer to the following talk.

(1) Who is the speaker?
(A) A student. (B) An English teacher.
(C) A Chinese teacher. (D) A shop clerk.

(2) What is suggested about the listeners?
(A) They want to learn how to write Chinese.
(B) They want to learn how to speak Chinese.
(C) They can speak Chinese well.
(D) They are studying English conversation.

[2] Questions (3) and (4) refer to the following announcement.

(3) Where are the participants?
(A) In a vegetable shop. (B) In a school.
(C) In a community center. (D) In a garden.

(4) What will the participants do at 10 A.M.?
(A) Plant potatoes. (B) Have a rest.
(C) Make a path. (D) Have lunch.

Reading Section Practice

Part 1

Each sentence has a space where a word or phrase is missing. Choose the best answer to complete the sentence.

(1) Ms. White enjoyed __________ last Sunday.
(A) days (B) one day (C) daily (D) swimming

(2) The store is open twenty-four hours __________.
(A) a day (B) days (C) one day (D) daily

(3) John __________ smoking after several tries.
(A) gives to (B) gave from (C) gives in (D) gave up

(4) Students must submit their portfolio __________ week during the semester.
(A) one (B) each (C) all (D) per

(5) At first, Paul __________ to join our company.
(A) avoided (B) denied (C) imagined (D) intended

(6) They decided __________ the concert in the end.
(A) postpone (B) to postpone (C) postponed (D) postponing

(7) Would you mind __________ for me while I'm travelling abroad?
(A) cover (B) to cover (C) covering (D) coverage

(8) The staff will clean the music studio on a __________ basis.
(A) regular (B) regularly (C) regulate (D) regulation

Part 2

Each of the short texts has three spaces where a word or phrase is missing. For each space, choose the best answer to complete the text.

[1] Questions (1) to (3) refer to the following advertisement.

> **Guitar Lessons**
>
> Adults & Children
> Beginner-Intermediate Levels
>
> Do you want [(1)] the guitar, but think it's too hard?
> Did you take lessons, but never got to play songs?
>
> Let's learn how to play the music and songs that you like [(2)]!
> There's no need to worry about getting upset about difficult theory. I will show you everything you need to know to get going immediately!
>
> The lesson fee is $20 [(3)].
> Contact Dave at: (206)001-0000

(1) (A) play	(B) to play	(C) playing	(D) player
(2) (A) is performing	(B) to perform	(C) performed	(D) has performed
(3) (A) in a day	(B) for fee	(C) on time	(D) per hour

[2] Questions (4) to (6) refer to the following advertisement.

> **Chez Moi**
>
> Chez Moi is a recreational French-style cooking school, set in the quiet town of Concord.
>
> Courses:
>
> Half-day or one-day courses are designed to suit beginners as well as experienced cooks.
>
> If you love [(4)], then our school is for you. We will [(5)] you to cook with imagination and passion. Courses will be held every [(6)] weekend.
>
> Please email us for more information. chezmoi@int.cook.com

(4) (A) cook	(B) cooked	(C) to be cooked	(D) cooking
(5) (A) inspire	(B) interesting	(C) instant	(D) instead
(6) (A) another	(B) other	(C) each	(D) all

Part 3

Texts such as notices, letters and instant messages are followed by two or three questions. Choose the best answer to each question.

[1] Questions (1) and (2) refer to the following advertisement.

Walkies!

Are you a busy working dog owner? Do you worry about your dog home alone all day? Let us help. We love walking dogs and have years of experience! We offer walks for all dogs in the Bishop Wood area. We will walk most dogs in groups, but individual walking sessions can be arranged. We also offer dog-training sessions.
Prices start from £10 for a 30-60 minute walk in a group. See our webpage for more details and a full price list. To make a reservation please call Jackie on 056 6089 788662 www.bishopstokewalkies.com

(1) Who is the advertisement for?
(A) People who like walking dogs
(B) People who need a dog walker
(C) People who want a new job
(D) People who want to buy a dog

(2) How can you make a booking?
(A) By visiting Bishop Wood
(B) By taking a training session
(C) By calling Jackie
(D) By visiting the webpage

[2] Questions (3) and (4) refer to the following online chat conversation.

Luke [8:22 P.M.]: Hi. It looks like good weather tomorrow. Do you want to go fishing?

Nick [8:29 P.M.]: Hello! Yes, I'd love to. I got a new fishing rod! What time shall we go?

Luke [8:40 P.M.]: How about I come and pick you up at 6 A.M.? It takes an hour to drive to the river. Can you wait for me near the train station?

Nick [8:45 P.M.]: Sure, and thanks. I'll bring tea. Oh and can I borrow a net? I lost mine and haven't bought a new one yet.

Luke [8:50 P.M.]: No problem! See you in the morning.

(3) How will they get to the river?
(A) By train
(B) In Nick's car
(C) By boat
(D) In Luke's car

(4) What does Nick need to buy?
(A) A fishing rod
(B) Hot drinks
(C) A fishing net
(D) A train ticket

Unit 3 Commuting

Grammar Target: How Questions

Vocabulary Check 12

Listen to the following sentences and fill in the blanks.

(a) Drunk driving is (   ).

(b) Don't forget to have your (   ) with you.

(c) Have you made a (   ) yet?

(d) I'd like to know how to (   ) a traffic jam.

(e) My driving license will (   ) next month.

(f) Hawaii is a popular tourist (   ).

Listening Section Practice

Part 1 13

[1] Choose the picture that the phrase or sentence best describes.

(A)

(B)

(C)

(D)

[2] Listen again to the sentence and fill in the blanks.

People (   ) (   ) on a (   ).

Part 2 14

[1] Listen to questions or statements. After each question or statement, you will hear and read four responses. Choose the best response.

(1) (A) In ten minutes. (B) It stops often.
(C) I don't stop. (D) In front of the bank.

(2) (A) Very well. (B) Two miles.
(C) Only half an hour. (D) It's here.

(3) (A) It's coming soon. (B) I'm fine.
(C) In the neighborhood. (D) I'm afraid not.

(4) (A) At seven thirty. (B) On foot.
(C) Twice a week. (D) On Wednesday.

(5) (A) That'll be a great help. (B) Yesterday morning.
(C) Yes, I am. (D) I ride it every day.

[2] Listen again to each question or statement and fill in the blanks.

(1) ( ) ( ) the bus stop?

(2) ( ) ( ) ( ) it ( ) to school from here?

(3) The ( ) network ( ) very nice in this area, ( ) ( )?

(4) ( ) ( ) you ( ) to school?

(5) ( ) you ( ) ( ) ( )?

Part 3 15

Listen to some short conversations. You will hear and read two questions about each conversation. Choose the best answer to each question.

[1] Questions (1) and (2) refer to the following conversation.

(1) What does the woman want to borrow?
(A) A phone. (B) A key. (C) A book. (D) A bicycle.

(2) When does the man expect the bike back?
(A) By twelve o'clock. (B) Until now.
(C) In the evening. (D) Tomorrow.

[2] Questions (3) and (4) refer to the following conversation.

(3) How long does it take to get to the theatre?
(A) Within a minute. (B) Three minutes.
(C) Five minutes. (D) Ten minutes.

(4) How will the man probably get to his destination?
(A) By bus. (B) By taxi. (C) By train. (D) By bike.

Part 4 16

Listen to some short talks. You will hear and read two questions about each talk. Choose the best answer to each question.

[1] Questions (1) and (2) refer to the following announcement.

(1) Why will the train to London be late?
(A) The platform has changed.
(B) It will leave at 9:25.
(C) There are no passengers.
(D) The weather is bad.

(2) What time will the train to Manchester depart?
(A) From Platform 3.
(B) At 9:15.
(C) From Platform 2.
(D) At 9:37.

[2] Questions (3) and (4) refer to the following radio announcement.

(3) How is the weather?
(A) Fine.
(B) Cloudy.
(C) Sunny.
(D) Rainy.

(4) Why is there a long traffic jam?
(A) There was a crash.
(B) The road is under construction.
(C) Cars are moving slowly.
(D) The city is 2 kilometers away.

Reading Section Practice

Part 1

Each sentence has a space where a word or phrase is missing. Choose the best answer to complete the sentence.

(1) It __________ about two hours to arrive at the airport.
(A) take (B) takes (C) taken (D) taking

(2) Mr. Adams __________ a gift for his son on his way home.
(A) buy (B) is bought (C) bought (D) buying

(3) Please __________ in advance when you take trains.
(A) get (B) ride (C) have (D) pay

(4) There __________ a map of the city on the wall.
(A) is (B) are (C) have (D) go

(5) Please __________ sure to have all your belongings with you.
(A) take (B) keep (C) have (D) make

(6) This train is __________ for Tokyo.
(A) sound (B) round (C) found (D) bound

(7) If you are headed downtown, please __________ a detour.
(A) avoid (B) take (C) slow (D) stop

(8) Some radio stations __________ traffic information every few hours.
(A) offer (B) offers (C) is offered (D) offering

Strategies for TOEIC BRIDGE #2

Reading Part 1 – Sentence Completion

There are 15 grammar and vocabulary focused questions in this section. Try to scan the sentences first for meaning. Do not spend too much time on any one question, as you will lose time for other potentially easier questions later.

Part 2

Each of the short texts has three spaces where a word or phrase is missing. For each space, choose the best answer to complete the text.

[1] Questions (1) to (3) refer to the following letter.

Dear employer,

Please [(1)] our apology for the late arrival of your employee traveling on TU Commuting Service, bus number 324 on May 15 in the morning. This bus was delayed [(2)] of mechanical problems. If you have any questions or [(3)], please call us at 1-800-000-000.

Greg Hamilton
Customer Service Representative

(1) (A) forget (B) accept (C) make (D) assist

(2) (A) in front (B) in charge (C) in spite (D) because

(3) (A) give explanation (B) tell your situation
(C) need specific information (D) ignore opinions

[2] Questions (4) to (6) refer to the following notice.

REMINDER: RENEWING THE PARKING PERMIT

It is the holders' [(4)] to renew their parking permit before the expiration date. You are obliged to [(5)] a penalty if you park your car in the parking space for the holders and your permit has been expired for more than three days.

Please make sure you renew your permit [(6)]. If you have an online account and follow the instructions, your permit card will be renewed digitally within a few seconds. For those who do not have an account, check our website and register for a new online account.

(4) (A) disability (B) priority (C) responsibility (D) stability

(5) (A) pay (B) be paid (C) paid (D) paying

(6) (A) as soon as the permit expires (B) while the permit expired
(C) after the day of expiration (D) before the expiry date

Part 3

Texts such as notices, letters and instant messages are followed by two or three questions. Choose the best answer to each question.

[1] Questions (1) and (2) refer to the following text message.

Rachel [12:20 P.M.]

Hi, Lisa! I missed the bus, so I have to come by bike. But I've got a flat tire which I need to fix. I'm going to be late. Sorry. I'll be there by 1 P.M. Where shall we meet, at your office or in the restaurant?

Lisa [12:24 P.M.]

____

(1) What will Rachel do?
(A) Catch the bus
(B) Repair her bicycle
(C) Work late
(D) Arrive early

(2) Select the best response to Rachel's message.
(A) "OK, I'll see you tomorrow."
(B) "Thanks, I'll catch the bus."
(C) "Yes, I will be working."
(D) "OK, I'll wait in the restaurant."

[2] Questions (3) and (4) refer to the following instructions.

How to hire a bicycle.

First download the Rentabike app. Fill in the online form and input your credit card details. There is no need to make a reservation.

Go to the nearest bicycle collection point with your credit card and touch the screen to begin.

Choose 'Rent Bike' and take the printed code to unlock your bike. The first 30 minutes is £2 .50 and then £1 for every extra 30 minutes.

(3) What do you need to do to rent a bicycle?
(A) Download an app
(B) Pay a deposit
(C) Pay in advance
(D) Make a reservation

(4) How much will it cost to rent a bicycle for two hours?
(A) £2.50
(B) £3.50
(C) £4.50
(D) £5.50

Unit 4 Fashion

Grammar Target: Present Continuous

Vocabulary Check 17

Listen to the following sentences and fill in the blanks.

(a) Your (　　　　　) is (　　　　　).

(b) This shirt is (　　　　　) (　　　　　) (　　　　　) (　　　　　).

(c) Do you have (　　　　　) (　　　　　) color in (　　　　　) sizes?

(d) I (　　　　　) to wear (　　　　　) clothes.

(e) Students are (　　　　　) to wear (　　　　　) (　　　　　).

(f) Please (　　　　　) the (　　　　　) (　　　　　) if you join the party.

Listening Section Practice

Part 1 18

[1] Choose the picture that the phrase or sentence best describes.

(A)

(B)

(C)

(D)

[2] Listen again to the sentence and fill in the blanks.

A man (　　　　　) (　　　　　) (　　　　　) a (　　　　　).

Part 2 19

[1] Listen to questions or statements. After each question or statement, you will hear and read four responses. Choose the best response.

(1) (A) I look at the window. (B) You may.
(C) No, I don't have it. (D) Great.

(2) (A) Did I? (B) Yes, it's yours.
(C) Thank you. (D) How much is it?

(3) (A) I'm making it. (B) Of course, I do.
(C) It's a warehouse. (D) I have a job interview.

(4) (A) School is closed. (B) Next week.
(C) I'm selling them. (D) It's on sale.

(5) (A) I bought it yesterday. (B) Yes, I will.
(C) At once. (D) At the second hand store.

[2] Listen again to each question or statement and fill in the blanks.

(1) (　　　　) (　　　　) I (　　　　)?
(2) I (　　　　) (　　　　) (　　　　) (　　　　).
(3) (　　　　) (　　　　) you (　　　　) a suit?
(4) (　　　　) (　　　　) you (　　　　) a school (　　　　)?
(5) (　　　　) (　　　　) you (　　　　) that nice (　　　　)?

Part 3 20

Listen to some short conversations. You will hear and read two questions about each conversation. Choose the best answer to each question.

[1] Questions (1) and (2) refer to the following conversation.

(1) What color jacket is the man going to wear?
(A) Blue. (B) Green. (C) Gray. (D) Black.

(2) Where will the man go?
(A) To an interview. (B) To work. (C) To the theater. (D) To the tailor.

[2] Questions (3) and (4) refer to the following conversation.

(3) What does the woman plan to do?
(A) Look at the ad. (B) Use materials.
(C) Play winter sports. (D) Buy clothes.

(4) What concern does the man have about the shirt?
(A) The price. (B) The volume.
(C) The texture. (D) The color.

There is no substitute for hard work.
[Thomas Edison]

Part 4 21

Listen to some short talks. You will hear and read two questions about each talk. Choose the best answer to each question.

[1] Questions (1) and (2) refer to the following conversation.

(1) Where are the ladies?
(A) In a shop. (B) In an office. (C) At school. (D) At home.

(2) What is the woman's concern about the sweater?
(A) The room. (B) The color. (C) The style. (D) The size.

[2] Questions (3) and (4) refer to the following talk.

(3) Who is the speaker?
(A) Anna Drew. (B) A graduate student.
(C) Peter Tilston. (D) Fashion show MC.

(4) What is the first model wearing?
(A) A long black dress. (B) Long silver earrings.
(C) Blue wool pants. (D) A silver evening dress.

Reading Section Practice

Part 1

Each sentence has a space where a word or phrase is missing. Choose the best answer to complete the sentence.

(1) Paul is ________ to have his haircut tomorrow.
(A) cutting (B) planning (C) fixing (D) wearing

(2) There is a wardrobe with ________ doors in the bedroom.
(A) stopping (B) stepping (C) slipping (D) sliding

(3) Jessica ordered ________ shoes from that store.
(A) a bundle of (B) a set of (C) a pair of (D) a piece of

(4) That red tie ________ very well with the suit.
(A) has (B) goes (C) comes (D) takes

(5) George is ________ his pants.
(A) supervising (B) yawning (C) recruiting (D) mending

(6) One of my favorite shirts is now ________ washed.
(A) being (B) having (C) taking (D) doing

(7) Why are you ________ that?
(A) wear (B) wears (C) wore (D) wearing

(8) Every participant ________ how to wear *kimono*.
(A) is selling (B) are studying (C) is learning (D) are taking

Part 2

Each of the short texts has three spaces where a word or phrase is missing. For each space, choose the best answer to complete the text.

[1] Questions (1) to (3) refer to the following letter.

Date:	15th October, 2019
Subject:	Farewell Party

Dear Colleagues,

You are [(1)] to a farewell party in honor of a valued colleague. John is [(2)] our company after 12 years of dedicated service.

Please join us on 22nd Friday starting at 7 p.m. to say goodbye to our beloved colleague and to express our best wishes for his new step.

Dress code for this farewell party is smart casual. Attendance is not compulsory. Please reply by Monday to let me know you [(3)] the party or not. Thank you.

Yours,
Human Resources
Mark Epstein

(1) (A) invite	(B) invited	(C) inviting	(D) invitation
(2) (A) coming	(B) going	(C) stopping	(D) leaving
(3) (A) are coming	(B) are inviting	(C) are enjoying	(D) are attending

[2] Questions (4) to (6) refer to the following instruction.

Return Policy

If you want to [(4)] a return, here is how:

<u>30-day Returns</u>

When you get your gear, you have 30 days to get it back to us.
If it does not [(5)] you, or you don't like it as much as you hoped, you can simply return it.
Please fill in the returns form and send it along with the gear.

<u>Extended Holiday Returns</u>

As we are [(6)] a Christmas sale during this season, any orders placed between November 15th and December 24th can be returned until January 31st.

(4) (A) make	(B) turn	(C) host	(D) tie
(5) (A) like	(B) fit	(C) tighten	(D) arrange
(6) (A) closing	(B) having	(C) getting	(D) waiting

Part 3

Texts such as notices, letters and instant messages are followed by two or three questions. Choose the best answer to each question.

[1] Questions (1) and (2) refer to the following notice.

Rules for hotel part-time workers.

1. You must wear the uniform
   Black pants (No stains or rips)
   Polo shirt (provided by the company)
   Clean sneakers (black, white or gray)
2. To keep the uniform clean at all times,
   make sure to wash the uniform (particularly the polo shirt) after each time worn.
3. To keep to the decided work time,
   if work finishes earlier than scheduled, please report to your supervisor.

(1) What will the company supply?
(A) Black pants
(B) Clean pants
(C) A polo shirt
(D) White sneakers

(2) What will they need to do when they get home?
(A) Report to their supervisor
(B) Wear a uniform
(C) Wash their polo shirt
(D) Call the hotel

[2] Questions (3) and (4) refer to the following text message.

Rachel: Hey there! I just got home late from the office. What are you wearing to Luke's party tonight?

Katie: Hey! ______________________________

(3) What will they do tonight?
(A) Work with Luke
(B) Go to the office
(C) Finish work
(D) Go to a party

(4) Select the best response to Rachel's message.
(A) "My new green dress."
(B) "I'll see you at the office."
(C) "I haven't finished yet."
(D) "Meet me at Luke's."

Unit 5 Personality

Grammar Target: Comparative and Superlative

Vocabulary Check 22

Listen to the following sentences and fill in the blanks.

(a) I (　　　　　) history (　　　　　) (　　　　　) science.

(b) Who got (　　　　　) (　　　　　) score on the (　　　　　)?

(c) Our teacher is getting (　　　　　) and (　　　　　) (　　　　　).

(d) My score is (　　　　　) (　　　　　) his.

(e) Be (　　　　　) to (　　　　　) (　　　　　).

(f) You can (　　　　　) (　　　　　) the (　　　　　) later.

Listening Section Practice

Part 1 23

[1] Choose the picture that the phrase or sentence best describes.

(A)

(B)

(C)

(D)

[2] Listen again to the sentence and fill in the blanks.

Students (　　　　　) (　　　　　) a (　　　　　).

Part 2 24

[1] Listen to questions or statements. After each question or statement, you will hear and read four responses. Choose the best response.

(1) (A) I like it. (B) Yes, it's better.
(C) No, it's not important. (D) I like both.

(2) (A) Mr. Martin does. (B) Yesterday.
(C) It was the last quarter. (D) In the classroom.

(3) (A) So do I. (B) The best player.
(C) No, it's not yours. (D) She's in my class, too.

(4) (A) It's in my class. (B) Me, too.
(C) No, you don't. (D) The first one.

(5) (A) He is lucky. (B) It's a film score.
(C) Congratulations. (D) He's a math teacher.

[2] Listen again to each question or statement and fill in the blanks.

(1) (   ) do you (   ) (   ), science or history?
(2) (   ) (   ) you (   ) this semester?
(3) I (   ) the music class (   ) (   ).
(4) I'm (   ) (   ) (   ) literature (   ) science.
(5) I got (   ) (   ) score on the math (   ).

Part 3 25

Listen to some short conversations. You will hear and read two questions about each conversation. Choose the best answer to each question.

[1] Questions (1) and (2) refer to the following conversation.

(1) How does the man look?
(A) Sad. (B) Angry. (C) Energetic. (D) Sleepy.

(2) Who is Mr. Taylor?
(A) A student. (B) A teacher. (C) A musician. (D) A politician.

[2] Questions (3) and (4) refer to the following conversation and score sheet.

<Your Results>

Subject	Your Score	Average Score
Math	77	55
English	91	62
Science	80	64
History	80	68
Spanish	62	65

(3) What is the woman's favorite subject?
(A) Math. (B) English. (C) Science. (D) History.

(4) What subject did the woman fail?
(A) Math. (B) Science. (C) History. (D) Spanish.

Part 4 26

Listen to some short talks. You will hear and read two questions about each talk. Choose the best answer to each question.

[1] Questions (1) and (2) refer to the following talk.

(1) What do students need to do to borrow books?
(A) Visit the study area.
(B) Make an ID card.
(C) Turn off their phone.
(D) Be quiet.

(2) What will students do next?
(A) Borrow books from the library
(B) Take a photo
(C) Make an ID card
(D) Take a tour of the library

[2] Questions (3) and (4) refer to the following voice message.

(3) Why will Rachel submit homework next week?
(A) She was sick.
(B) She didn't finish it.
(C) She didn't have the print outs.
(D) She didn't understand it.

(4) What is suggested about the class last week?
(A) It was too easy.
(B) There wasn't any homework.
(C) It was difficult.
(D) They read a lot of books.

Reading Section Practice

Part 1

Each sentence has a space where a word or phrase is missing. Choose the best answer to complete the sentence.

(1) Paul speaks French __________ Michel.
(A) fluency (B) most fluent (C) more fluently (D) as fluently as

(2) Most students agree Mrs. Evans is __________ teacher in school.
(A) interesting (B) more interested
(C) the most interesting (D) as interesting as

(3) Ms. Winehouse is nominated for __________ teacher award.
(A) the better (B) the less (C) the best (D) the most

(4) __________ you practice, the faster you solve problems.
(A) Well (B) The more (C) Best (D) The most

(5) Arabic is __________ any other language for me.
(A) such difficult to (B) more difficult than (C) most difficult of (D) difficult as

(6) The lecturer got __________ excited as he went on.
(A) as well as (B) much more (C) more and more (D) best

(7) George worked __________ than I.
(A) hard (B) harder (C) hardly (D) the hardest

(8) Dr. Smith has twice as __________ books as I.
(A) many (B) large (C) much (D) lot

Part 2

Each of the short texts has three spaces where a word or phrase is missing. For each space, choose the best answer to complete the text.

[1] Questions (1) to (3) refer to the following instruction.

Debate Rules

If you want to be [(1)] familiar with debate, the following is the [(2)] basic style of debate structure you should know.

First, group A has three minutes to present their case to the audience. Then group B has three minutes to present their case. Second, both groups receive three minutes to prepare a rebuttal. Group B now is the first to refute, and group A will be the second.

The more you practice, the [(3)] you get at debating.

(1) (A) more	(B) less	(C) much	(D) least
(2) (A) good	(B) well	(C) more	(D) most
(3) (A) good	(B) well	(C) better	(D) best

[2] Questions (4) to (6) refer to the following note.

For educators,

Rules are one of the [(4)] aspects of every classroom. They have a tremendous effect on kids, especially teenagers.

At the beginning of each academic year, you should go over the rules in class with all your students. Students are [(5)] likely to follow the rules when they understand the purpose behind them. Rules that seem to be unnecessary are often ignored. For this reason, it is important for both you and your students to communicate [(6)] you have established those rules and how those rules will help create a good classroom.

(4) (A) important	(B) importantly	(C) more important	(D) most important
(5) (A) well	(B) better	(C) more	(D) much
(6) (A) what	(B) when	(C) how	(D) why

Part 3

Texts such as notices, letters and instant messages are followed by two or three questions. Choose the best answer to each question.

[1] Questions (1) and (2) refer to the following advertisement.

Beginners Italian Class

Evening class for adults to learn the basics.

Wednesday - 7 P.M. to 8:30 P.M.
Start: 9th of September.   Course Length: 8 Weeks

Details of the course content and fees on www.communitycollegeoaklane.co.uk. Textbooks will be provided. If interested, please call the office between 6 P.M. and 7 P.M. to apply.

(1) Who is the class for?
(A) People who can speak Italian
(B) Children who want to learn Italian
(C) People from Italy
(D) Adults who can't speak Italian

(2) How can people join the course?
(A) By bringing a textbook
(B) By registering online
(C) By phoning the college
(D) By reading about the content

[2] Questions (3) and (4) refer to the following text message.

Jane: Hi, Terry. I'm trying to print my assignment but my computer has broken. Can I borrow yours?

Terry: ______________________________

(3) What does Jane ask Terry to do?
(A) Lend her a computer
(B) Print her assignment
(C) Borrow her printer
(D) Repair her computer

(4) Select the best response to Jane's message
(A) "This assignment is easy!"
(B) "I don't have a printer."
(C) "I haven't finished my assignment."
(D) "Sure. Come on over!"

Unit 6 Sleep

Grammar Target: Prepositions of Time

Vocabulary Check

27

Listen to the following sentences and fill in the blanks.

(a) ( ) ( ) your ( ) ( ) in bed.

(b) ( ) ( ) ( ) the TV ( ), please?

(c) I was ( ) ( ) ( ) the job interview.

(d) He ( ) ( ) ( ) in the shade.

(e) Here are ( ) ( ) ( ) for your child.

(f) You need to ( ) your cats again ( ) ( ).

Listening Section Practice

Part 1 28

[1] Choose the picture that the phrase or sentence best describes.

(A)

(B)

(C)

(D)

[2] Listen again to the sentence and fill in the blanks.

A woman is ( ) ( ) ( ).

Part 2 29

[1] Listen to questions or statements. After each question or statement, you will hear and read four responses. Choose the best response.

(1) (A) In six hours. (B) For seven times.
(C) After dinner. (D) At eleven thirty.

(2) (A) In the office. (B) After lunch.
(C) I didn't meet him. (D) It's on time.

(3) (A) That's right. (B) The lecturer is.
(C) Don't you? (D) For two hours.

(4) (A) He snores constantly. (B) It's nine o'clock.
(C) Not really. (D) He's half-asleep.

(5) (A) The car was wrecked. (B) He was in the garden.
(C) No, it wasn't. (D) My son was.

[2] Listen again to each question or statement and fill in the blanks.

(1) ( ) ( ) ( ) you ( ) to bed last night?
(2) ( ) ( ) the meeting ( )?
(3) The lecture ( ) at noon, ( ) ( )?
(4) ( ) you ( ) a ( ) ( )?
(5) ( ) ( ) in the car ( )?

Strategies for TOEIC BRIDGE #3

Listening Part 2 – Question-Response

In this section you will hear a question and four responses to it. Try to read the choices in the test book before listening. You can choose the correct answer before every choice is read out.

It is important to listen very carefully to the first part of the sentence to determine what kind of question it is. Is it a do/are (yes/no), where, what, who, or how question?

Part 3 30

Listen to some short conversations. You will hear and read two questions about each conversation. Choose the best answer to each question.

[1] Questions (1) and (2) refer to the following conversation.

(1) Who is the man?
(A) A clerk. (B) A doctor. (C) A patient. (D) A customer.

(2) What will the woman probably do next?
(A) Make a phone call. (B) Buy a bed.
(C) Look at a mirror. (D) Choose a pillow.

[2] Questions (3) and (4) refer to the following conversation.

(3) How is the man?
(A) He is energetic. (B) He is exhausted. (C) He is sad. (D) He is satisfied.

(4) What did the man do last night?
(A) He examined the bed. (B) He was sick in bed.
(C) He studied for the test. (D) He slept a lot.

Part 4 31

Listen to some short talks. You will hear and read two questions about each talk. Choose the best answer to each question.

[1] Question (1) and (2) refer to the following radio program.

(1) What is the book about?
(A) How to open a studio.
(B) How to stop drinking tea.
(C) How to sleep well.
(D) How to keep cool.

(2) What does the woman want to know?
(A) What Lewis did last week.
(B) When Lewis drinks coffee.
(C) Where Lewis sleeps.
(D) Why Lewis wrote the book.

[2] Questions (3) and (4) refer to the following telephone message.

(3) What will Linda do when she gets home?
(A) Do the laundry.
(B) Cook dinner.
(C) Phone Jane and Paul.
(D) Work from home.

(4) When will the man go shopping?
(A) Before work.
(B) When he gets home.
(C) At 7 P.M.
(D) After work.

Reading Section Practice

Part 1

Each sentence has a space where a word or phrase is missing. Choose the best answer to complete the sentence.

(1) Mark brushed his teeth ________ going to bed.
(A) in front (B) after (C) before (D) while

(2) Jane usually listens to the radio ________ getting ready for bed.
(A) during (B) behind (C) awhile (D) while

(3) Everyone was worried if John arrived at the airport ________ time.
(A) from (B) in (C) after (D) off

(4) What did you do ________ the weekend?
(A) when (B) from (C) on (D) since

(5) It is getting cold ________ night.
(A) at (B) than (C) on (D) in

(6) Joan is always up ________ dawn.
(A) in (B) prior (C) on (D) before

(7) It's five ________ eleven.
(A) when (B) in (C) through (D) past

(8) He went into the bedroom ten minutes ________.
(A) ago (B) before (C) left (D) right

Part 2

Each of the short texts has three spaces where a word or phrase is missing. For each space, choose the best answer to complete the text.

[1] Questions (1) to (3) refer to the following notice.

YARD SALE!

Sunday, May 12
8:00 A.M. to 4:00 P.M.

University Village [(1)] its annual village-wide yard sale. Many residents are [(2)] this big sale. So come and spend a wonderful day shopping for books, clothes, and furniture [(3)] beds and tables.

Parking space available. For more information, call 1-800-206-52.

(1) (A) is having	(B) is coming	(C) is going	(D) is taking
(2) (A) entering in	(B) sitting in	(C) looking in	(D) participating in
(3) (A) making	(B) sleeping	(C) including	(D) adding

[2] Questions (4) to (6) refer to the following article.

Some Hints for Better Sleep

Here are some tips for those who have problems with sleeping. It is said that 30% of adults sleep less than 5 hours a night.

Let's resolve problems [(4)] going to bed. First, do not consume alcohol or caffeine [(5)] two hours of bedtime. Second, turn off your cell phone at bedtime. It is not a good idea to use a laptop in bed either. Your bed should be used only for sleep! Finally, [(6)] in bed, avoid watching the clock. What you really need is to relax.

(4) (A) not	(B) after	(C) beyond	(D) before
(5) (A) with	(B) withdraw	(C) without	(D) within
(6) (A) once	(B) beneath	(C) over	(D) last

There are no gains without pains.
[Benjamin Franklin]

Part 3

Texts such as notices, letters and instant messages are followed by two or three questions. Choose the best answer to each question.

[1] Questions (1) and (2) refer to the following notice.

Eastwood Running Club

Pre-breakfast run every Monday, Wednesday and Friday
Start Time : 6:30 A.M.
Meeting place: East Oak School bus stop

In case of bad weather, the meet will be canceled. Please check the webpage for updates, which will be made by 6 A.M. No application is needed. For more information and practical running advice, please check our guidelines on www.eastwoodrunclub.asdf.org.

(1) When will participants go running?
(A) Before school
(B) At 6 A.M.
(C) Before breakfast
(D) After breakfast

(2) What will happen if it rains?
(A) They will run inside.
(B) They will meet later.
(C) They will wear raincoats.
(D) They won't go running.

[2] Questions (3) and (4) refer to the following e-mail.

Date:	Sunday, 9th July
Subject:	Instructions for feeding Charlie

Dear Anne,

Thanks for taking care of our cat while we are away. We will be leaving this evening. We'll feed him before we go. We'll be back on Friday.
Please feed him once in the morning and again in the evening. Our neighbor will also visit him during the day. First make sure he has water. Then give him some of the dried food. Make sure he eats it all. After he finishes he can have the fresh food. Finally please wash his food bowl.

Thanks again,
Claire

(3) Who is Charlie?
(A) The cat
(B) The neighbor
(C) The friend
(D) The cat owner

(4) What will Ann do last?
(A) Feed the cat fresh food
(B) Give the cat water
(C) Check he finished the dried food
(D) Wash the cat's dish

Unit 7 Travel

Grammar Target: Future Tense

Vocabulary Check 32

Listen to the following sentences and fill in the blanks.

(a) All (　　　　　) are going to be (　　　　　) due to the snow.

(b) I need to (　　　　　) my (　　　　　).

(c) I'll (　　　　　) (　　　　　) to (　　　　　) your country.

(d) He is going to (　　　　　) (　　　　　) on business.

(e) The (　　　　　) is (　　　　　) our (　　　　　).

(f) This ship's (　　　　　) is Paris.

Listening Section Practice

Part 1 33

[1] Choose the picture that the phrase or sentence best describes.

(A)

(B)

(C)

(D)

[2] Listen again to the sentence and fill in the blanks.

A man (　　　　　) (　　　　　) a (　　　　　).

Part 2 34

[1] Listen to questions or statements. After each question or statement, you will hear and read four responses. Choose the best response.

(1) (A) On holidays. (B) He's English.
(C) To France. (D) To do my homework.

(2) (A) Good job. (B) It's gone.
(C) Me, too. (D) Ok, I will.

(3) (A) Yes, you did. (B) Yes, you are.
(C) I will support you. (D) It's filled.

(4) (A) Yes, I've been there. (B) No, you're not.
(C) They're mine. (D) Yes, I'm excited.

(5) (A) I'll turn on the radio. (B) No wonder it's cold outside.
(C) I'll go at night. (D) Yes, it's not cold.

[2] Listen again to each question or statement and fill in the blanks.

(1) (　　　　) (　　　　) you (　　　　) on your next (　　　　)?
(2) (　　　　) (　　　　) (　　　　) volunteer to (　　　　) the panda?
(3) (　　　　) (　　　　) to (　　　　) (　　　　) this form, right?
(4) (　　　　) (　　　　) to meet your (　　　　), (　　　　) (　　　　)?
(5) The radio says (　　　　) (　　　　) (　　　　) (　　　　) tonight.

Part 3 35

Listen to some short conversations. You will hear and read two questions about each conversation. Choose the best answer to each question.

[1] Questions (1) and (2) refer to the following conversation.

(1) What is the man going to do in the evening?
(A) Cook French food. (B) Learn French.
(C) Go shopping. (D) Eat French food.

(2) When is the man going to France?
(A) In the morning. (B) In the evening. (C) Tomorrow. (D) In two days.

[2] Questions (3) and (4) refer to the following conversation and price list.

Round-Trip Price List

Seattle-Paris	$1100
Seattle-Mexico City	$600
Seattle-Hong Kong	$1200
Seattle-Tokyo	$750

(3) What does the woman want to do?
(A) Go to an airport. (B) Visit Asia. (C) Make a budget. (D) Ask the seller.

(4) Which city does the man recommend to visit?
(A) Paris. (B) Mexico City. (C) Hong Kong. (D) Tokyo.

Part 4 36

Listen to some short talks. You will hear and read two questions about each talk. Choose the best answer to each question.

[1] Questions (1) and (2) refer to the following announcement.

(1) Who are the listeners?
(A) Pilots. (B) Ground staff. (C) Air stewards. (D) Passengers.

(2) Why is take off delayed?
(A) The weather is bad. (B) There is no entertainment.
(C) The pilot is late. (D) They are ten minutes late.

[2] Questions (3) and (4) refer to the following voice message.

(3) How many nights are the customers going to stay in the hotel?
(A) One night. (B) Two nights. (C) Three nights. (D) Four nights.

(4) Why does the listener need to call the hotel?
(A) To confirm the reservation. (B) To pay for the room.
(C) To change the dates. (D) To cancel the booking.

Reading Section Practice

Part 1

Each sentence has a space where a word or phrase is missing. Choose the best answer to complete the sentence.

(1) This plane is going to take off in a few minutes as ________.
(A) mentioned (B) invested (C) destined (D) scheduled

(2) One of Ms. Hill's hobbies ________ learning foreign languages.
(A) is (B) are (C) have (D) take

(3) This is the train ________ for Hakata.
(A) round (B) found (C) sound (D) bound

(4) Today a lot of people ________ plane tickets online.
(A) travel (B) note (C) book (D) pen

(5) The airplane is going to be ________ due to the storm.
(A) purchased (B) slowly (C) lately (D) delayed

(6) I'd like to ________ my reservation.
(A) recite (B) recess (C) rent (D) reconfirm

(7) Are you going to ________ all of your Japanese yen into dollars?
(A) convert (B) subvert (C) pervert (D) expert

(8) I'm going to ________ a few hours at the airport lounge.
(A) depend (B) spend (C) rend (D) suspend

Part 2

Each of the short texts has three spaces where a word or phrase is missing. For each space, choose the best answer to complete the text.

[1] Questions (1) to (3) refer to the following instruction.

Life Jacket Instructions

First, [(1)] life jacket over your head with the reflecting tapes facing outward. Second, press the strap around your back and secure the buckle. Third, pull the strap tight and [(2)] collar laces. It is going to [(3)] a few seconds for the jacket to inflate after pulling the safety plug.

(1) (A) flight	(B) aboard	(C) wearing	(D) place
(2) (A) strengthen	(B) fasten	(C) forgotten	(D) thicken
(3) (A) spend	(B) take	(C) let	(D) make

[2] Questions (4) to (6) refer to the following instruction.

Happy Travel Insurance Co.
111 Madison St.
Maple Leaf Pl. 98001

Instructions for Baggage Lost, Damaged or Stolen Claim

The Baggage Expense Claim Form can be used to file claims for:

- Items lost, stolen or damaged [(4)] your trip
- Items you purchased when your luggage was delayed or [(5)] by an airline

Please fill out the Baggage Expense Claim Form and return it with the documentation listed below.

For all claims, submit

- Copies of your travel documents confirming your travel dates and [(6)].
- Copies of receipts for all claimed baggage expenses.
- Proof of payment of the claimed baggage expenses.

Your claim must be submitted to the address at the top of these instructions.

(4) (A) during	(B) while	(C) between	(D) behind
(5) (A) misunderstood	(B) mistook	(C) misrouted	(D) mister
(6) (A) history	(B) itinerary	(C) story	(D) memory

Part 3

Texts such as notices, letters and instant messages are followed by two or three questions. Choose the best answer to each question.

[1] Questions (1) and (2) refer to the following notice.

ROOM INFORMATION

Newspapers will be delivered every morning before 7 A.M.

Breakfast is served between 6 A.M. and 10 A.M. in the Green Room. Room service is available 24 hrs. Menu is in the bedside drawer.

Hotel rooms will be cleaned daily between 11 A.M. and 2 P.M. If you do not want your room cleaned, please leave the sign on the door.

If you need fresh towels, leave the old towels on the bathroom floor.

(1) Who is the notice for?
(A) Hotel staff (B) Guests (C) Students (D) Cleaners

(2) What time will cleaners work in the rooms?
(A) From 6 A.M. to 10 A.M. (B) Before 7 A.M.
(C) From 11 A.M. to 2 P.M. (D) After 2 P.M.

[2] Questions (3) and (4) refer to the following text message.

Sally: Hi, Jenny. Are you busy on Saturday night? I'm going to be in town for a meeting in the morning. I thought we could hang out in the evening, maybe go out to eat? Is it OK if I stay at yours?

Jenny: ______________________________

(3) Where most likely will they go Saturday night?
(A) To the office (B) To a restaurant
(C) To a meeting (D) To a friend's house

(4) Select the best response to Sally's message.
(A) "Sure. See you tonight!"
(B) "Yes, I'm really busy these days."
(C) "Sure, I'll look forward to seeing you!"
(D) "Yes, I can stay for the meeting."

Unit 8 Diets

Grammar Target: Present Perfect Tense

Vocabulary Check 37

Listen to the following sentences and fill in the blanks.

(a) (   ) (   ) (   ) raw fish.
(b) (   ) calling to (   ) your (   ).
(c) (   ) you (   ) breakfast (   )?
(d) (   ) you (   ) to (   )?
(e) You (   ) (   ) a party plan for 20 people.
(f) We (   ) (   ) a lot of dishes.

Listening Section Practice

Part 1 38

[1] Choose the picture that the phrase or sentence best describes.

(A)

(B)

(C)

(D)

[2] Listen again to the sentence and fill in the blanks.

Some (   ) are in the (   ).

Part 2 39

[1] Listen to questions or statements. After each question or statement, you will hear and read four responses. Choose the best response.

(1) (A) I like to eat. (B) Your lunch is ready.
(C) No, I have one. (D) No, not yet.

(2) (A) Yes, I am. (B) I hope you like beans.
(C) No, I haven't been there. (D) Since I was twenty.

(3) (A) Yes, it's in order. (B) The lady on your right.
(C) I need more time. (D) I've never been ready.

(4) (A) You should try it. (B) Before dinner.
(C) You never know. (D) Yes, I do.

(5) (A) At eight tonight. (B) I'm happy you enjoyed it.
(C) I've had enough. (D) I'll be ready.

[2] Listen again to each question or statement and fill in the blanks.

(1) Hi Jake, (   ) you (   ) lunch (   )?
(2) (   ) (   ) (   ) you (   ) a vegan?
(3) (   ) you (   ) to (   )?
(4) (   ) (   ) (   ) *sashimi* before.
(5) (   ) you (   ) the wonderful dinner.

Part 3 40

Listen to some short conversations. You will hear and read two questions about each conversation. Choose the best answer to each question.

[1] Questions (1) and (2) refer to the following conversation.

(1) When is breakfast served?
(A) At 5:30 A.M. (B) At 6:00 A.M. (C) At 6:30 A.M. (D) At 10:00 A.M.

(2) Where are the speakers?
(A) At a library. (B) At a diner.
(C) At a hotel. (D) At a supermarket.

[2] Questions (3) and (4) refer to the following conversation.

(3) Where does the conversation take place?
(A) At a cafe. (B) At a hospital. (C) At a warehouse. (D) At an office.

(4) What will the woman do next?
(A) Order a burger. (B) Quit being a vegan.
(C) Ask for water. (D) Smell a beef burger.

If you can dream it, you can do it.
[Walt Disney]

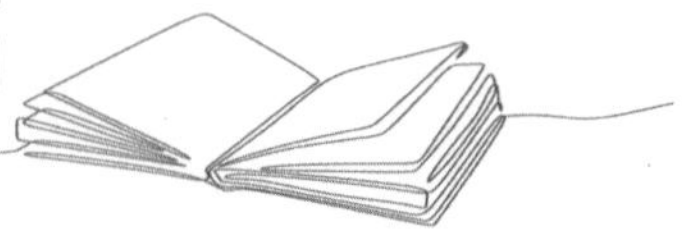

Part 4 41

Listen to some short talks. You will hear and read two questions about each talk. Choose the best answer to each question.

[1] Questions (1) and (2) refer to the following phone message.

(1) What is Ms. Heslop planning?
(A) An evening dinner for 20.
(B) A romantic dinner for two.
(C) A special birthday lunch.
(D) An Indian cooking lesson.

(2) What is suggested about the party guests?
(A) All of them are meat eaters.
(B) Some of them are vegetarian.
(C) All of them are vegetarian.
(D) None of them like Indian food.

[2] Questions (3) and (4) refer to the following talk.

(3) Who is the speaker?
(A) A cook.
(B) A blogger.
(C) A YouTuber.
(D) A radio announcer.

(4) What did he learn to do?
(A) To use a computer.
(B) To cook healthy food.
(C) To give advice.
(D) To write a blog.

Reading Section Practice

Part 1

Each sentence has a space where a word or phrase is missing. Choose the best answer to complete the sentence.

(1) We haven't _________ breakfast yet.
(A) have (B) has (C) had (D) having

(2) _________ everyone on the team taken a lunch break?
(A) Have (B) Has (C) Is (D) Does

(3) Some of the clients _________ just called to say that they will be late for the dinner.
(A) is (B) are (C) have (D) had

(4) Mr. Stein has just _________ the restaurant.
(A) leave (B) leaves (C) left (D) leaving

(5) I'm afraid you've already _________ too much.
(A) drink (B) drank (C) drunk (D) drinking

(6) I _________ that restaurant with my cousin two days ago.
(A) visit (B) visited (C) have visited (D) visiting

(7) All tables have already been _________ tonight.
(A) booked (B) took (C) cooked (D) shook

(8) Has anyone taken your order _________?
(A) still (B) just (C) but (D) yet

Part 2

Each of the short texts has three spaces where a word or phrase is missing. For each space, choose the best answer to complete the text.

[1] Questions (1) to (3) refer to the following notice.

Vegetarian Food Fair

It will showcase a wide (1) of authentic vegetarian dishes from all around the world.

Curry Rice, Mee Rebus, Spring Roll, Fried Carrot Cake and a lot more!

You have never (2) a veggie meal? That's fine! You'll learn how (3) cook, eat, and enjoy vegetarian food.

Date: Sunday June 28
Time: 11:00 - 14:00
Venue: Walden Buddhist Church, Lincoln St. 442

(1) (A) tiny	(B) witty	(C) anxiety	(D) variety
(2) (A) enjoy	(B) ate	(C) had	(D) been
(3) (A) to	(B) on	(C) in	(D) by

[2] Questions (4) to (6) refer to the following letter.

Hello Linda,

Thanks for (4) to the dinner party last night. I was very pleased that you liked the dishes and asked me for the recipe. I (5) the file for you. If you have any questions, please let me know. I'd (6) happy to help you. See you soon!

Yours,
Olivia

(4) (A) come	(B) came	(C) comer	(D) coming
(5) (A) attaches	(B) have attached	(C) attaching	(D) attachment
(6) (A) be	(B) do	(C) wil	(D) had

Part 3

Texts such as notices, letters and instant messages are followed by two or three questions. Choose the best answer to each question.

[1] Questions (1) and (2) refer to the following advertisement.

Beginners Cooking Class **Thursdays 6 P.M. - 8 P.M.**

In this six week course, you will learn the basics of cooking including how to plan meals for a week. We will supply all equipment and a recipe book. All ingredients are included in the fee. Please bring your own container to take food home with you. For more details, please check the webpage www.cookingskills.com and register online by September 14.

(1) What will people do before September 14?
- (A) Plan meals
- (B) Pay for the course
- (C) Begin to cook
- (D) Apply for the course

(2) What will they take to class?
- (A) Tupperware
- (B) Recipe book
- (C) Ingredients
- (D) An apron

[2] Questions (3) and (4) refer to the following text message.

Tom: Sorry, I'm late. I'm on my way home now. I got held up in a meeting. Have you already eaten?

Sarah: ______________________________

(3) Why is Tom late?
- (A) His work finished late.
- (B) He met old friends.
- (C) He went to the shop.
- (D) The train was late.

(4) Select the best response to Tom's message.
- (A) "I'm already at home."
- (B) "Where are you?"
- (C) "Did you cook?"
- (D) "No, not yet."

Unit 9 Money

Grammar Target: Auxiliary Verbs

Vocabulary Check 42

Listen to the following sentences and fill in the blanks.

(a) I'm going to (　　　　　) (　　　　　) (　　　　　).

(b) They are working on a (　　　　　) (　　　　　).

(c) I'd like to (　　　　　) (　　　　　) (　　　　　).

(d) I want to (　　　　　) (　　　　　) (　　　　　).

(e) The (　　　　　) (　　　　　) (　　　　　) is high.

(f) Money (　　　　　) (　　　　　) (　　　　　) soon.

Listening Section Practice

Part 1 43

[1] Choose the picture that the phrase or sentence best describes.

(A)

(B)

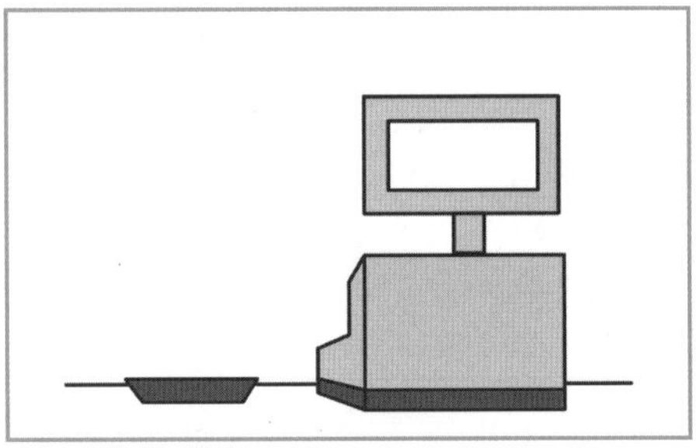

(C)

(D)

[2] Listen again to the sentence and fill in the blanks.

A (　　　　　) is (　　　　　) the new (　　　　　) (　　　　　).

Part 2 44

[1] Listen to questions or statements. After each question or statement, you will hear and read four responses. Choose the best response.

(1) (A) Thank you.
(B) To the left.
(C) She went away.
(D) It's been hot.

(2) (A) It was fun.
(B) She went shopping.
(C) I'm going next month.
(D) We'd better stop eating out.

(3) (A) It's ending.
(B) You meet your friend.
(C) I'm a manager.
(D) Good for you.

(4) (A) She's with me.
(B) I can lend you some money.
(C) On the wall.
(D) I bought it today.

(5) (A) Many times.
(B) I often do that.
(C) $100, please.
(D) Twice.

[2] Listen again to each question or statement and fill in the blanks.

(1) Here's an (   ) for you.
(2) We're (   ) a (   ) (   ) this month.
(3) I could (   ) (   ) (   ) (   ) this month.
(4) I don't (   ) my (   ) (   ) me today.
(5) (   ) (   ) would you like to (   ) to your savings account?

Part 3 45

Listen to some short conversations. You will hear and read two questions about each conversation. Choose the best answer to each question.

[1] Questions (1) and (2) refer to the following conversation.

(1) Where does the conversation take place?
(A) In a photo studio.
(B) In a bank.
(C) In a driving school.
(D) In a library.

(2) What does the woman show to the man?
(A) A license.
(B) A credit card.
(C) A passport.
(D) A photocopy.

[2] Questions (3) and (4) refer to the following conversation.

(3) Where is the woman going?
(A) America.
(B) Spain.
(C) Italy.
(D) France.

(4) What is the woman worried about?
(A) Weather.
(B) Prices.
(C) Language.
(D) Food.

Part 4 46

Listen to some short talks. You will hear and read two questions about each talk. Choose the best answer to each question.

[1] Questions (1) and (2) refer to the following announcement.

(1) How much is their regular hourly pay?
(A) $11.00. (B) $14.00. (C) $15.00. (D) $19.00.

(2) What will workers most likely do next?
(A) Submit bank account details. (B) Open a bank account.
(C) Deposit money. (D) Withdraw money.

[2] Questions (3) and (4) refer to the following announcement.

(3) How can listeners spend less?
(A) By eating out more. (B) Not buying food.
(C) By working more. (D) By making packed lunches.

(4) What should listeners do monthly?
(A) Spend their salary. (B) Open a new bank account.
(C) Deposit money into an account. (D) Work overtime.

Reading Section Practice

Part 1

Each sentence has a space where a word or phrase is missing. Choose the best answer to complete the sentence.

(1) You __________ not spend too much money before going on a trip.
(A) are (B) should (C) have (D) had

(2) You had __________ hurry to the ATM.
(A) nice (B) well (C) good (D) better

(3) __________ you check my saving account?
(A) Have (B) Had (C) Are (D) Will

(4) The estimated price for a new car is way over my __________.
(A) total (B) budget (C) choice (D) account

(5) He always thinks about the __________ market.
(A) stick (B) stroke (C) stroll (D) stock

(6) Ms. McCartney carefully checked the __________ of her account.
(A) balance (B) weight (C) stress (D) healthy

(7) We must __________ and not buy unnecessary clothes.
(A) ecology (B) economy (C) economize (D) economic

(8) George should __________ money to pay for his tuition.
(A) save (B) saves (C) saved (D) saving

Part 2

Each of the short texts has three spaces where a word or phrase is missing. For each space, choose the best answer to complete the text.

[1] Questions (1) to (3) refer to the following note.

TIPS TO AVOID IMPULSE-BUYING!

One: You should (1) your goals in mind!

Two: You must (2) a waiting period before you buy!

Three: You need to avoid shopping when you're excited!

Four: You (3) think of shopping as entertainment!

Try to do the tips above and you'll be able to save money.

(1) (A) keep	(B) keeps	(C) kept	(D) keeping
(2) (A) not	(B) be	(C) save	(D) have
(3) (A) not	(B) could not	(C) had not better	(D) should not

[2] Questions (4) to (6) refer to the following advertisement.

Our newly-improved light bulbs "ENEBulb" will (4) 9,000 hours of light and use much less of electricity (at 6 cents per kilowatt hour) than our old bulbs. To be exact, ENEBulb lasts 10 times longer and uses 70 percent less energy!

If you replace all bulbs in your house with our new bulbs, you will (5) about $60 a year. This is the easiest way to save money! (6) our "ENEBulb"!

(4) (A) is	(B) can	(C) must	(D) provide
(5) (A) consume	(B) spend	(C) save	(D) pay
(6) (A) Throw	(B) Try	(C) Turn	(D) Avoid

Strategies for TOEIC BRIDGE #4

Reading Part 2 – Text Completion

Similar to Part 1, this section focuses on grammar and vocabulary.
Try to read the direction such as "Questions 66 - 68 refer to *the letter*" before the text as it will prepare you for what you are going to read.

Part 3

Texts such as notices, letters and instant messages are followed by two or three questions. Choose the best answer to each question.

[1] Questions (1) and (2) refer to the following advertisement.

Bob's Warehouse

Spring Sale on all household items!

Special offer for buy now pay later kitchen deals. Order a new kitchen during the sale and receive a $500 discount. The first payment can be made after two months. 20% off all beds. 30% discounts on sofas and armchairs. Up to 40% off dining tables.

Sale starts Friday 5th June and finishes Monday 8th June.

Free ice cream for the kids, too!
Hurry up while the offer lasts!

(1) What does the store sell?
(A) Ice cream (B) Houses (C) Furniture (D) Cars

(2) How long will the sale continue?
(A) All spring (B) Four days (C) One week (D) Two months

[2] Questions (3) and (4) refer to the following text message.

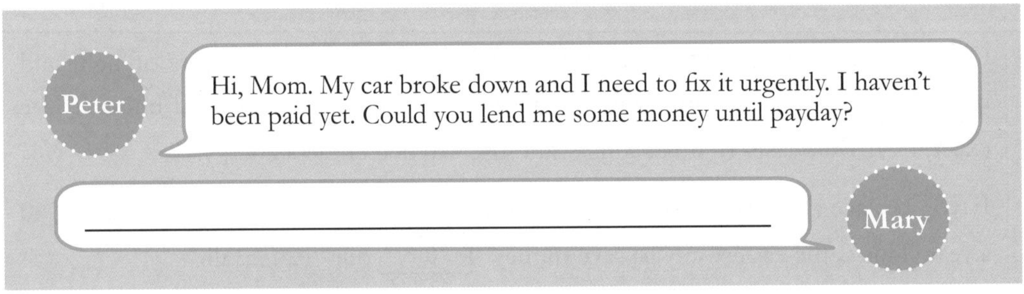

(3) What is Peter's problem?
(A) He doesn't have a job.
(B) He needs to lend some money.
(C) He doesn't have enough money.
(D) He needs to buy a car.

(4) Select the best response to Peter's message.
(A) "Yes, I've already been paid."
(B) "No, I don't have a car."
(C) "No, I didn't borrow any."
(D) "Sure, how much do you need?"

Unit 10 E-books

Grammar Target: Inanimate Subject

Vocabulary Check 47

Listen to the following sentences and fill in the blanks.

(a) I (　　　　) a (　　　　) (　　　　).

(b) You (　　　　) (　　　　) many books.

(c) I like (　　　　) (　　　　).

(d) I (　　　　) a (　　　　) (　　　　) at it.

(e) The heavy rain (　　　　) (　　　　) (　　　　) (　　　　) to the show.

(f) This book (　　　　) (　　　　) your (　　　　).

Listening Section Practice

Part 1 48

[1] Choose the picture that the phrase or sentence best describes.

(A)

(B)

(C)

(D)

[2] Listen again to the sentence and fill in the blanks.

A woman (　　　　) (　　　　) on the (　　　　).

Part 2 49

[1] Listen to questions or statements. After each question or statement, you will hear and read four responses. Choose the best response.

(1) (A) I bought it myself. (B) It is wonderful.
(C) Do you like it? (D) I have a free ticket.

(2) (A) It sounds interesting. (B) It's about time.
(C) I hope so, too. (D) In the society.

(3) (A) I was tired. (B) It takes hours.
(C) Oh, it's close. (D) They liked walking.

(4) (A) No, I wasn't. (B) Yes, it made me cry.
(C) You're listening. (D) It's a hard cover.

(5) (A) In front of the bus stop. (B) You showed me.
(C) It stopped raining. (D) I got a flat tire.

[2] Listen again to each question or statement and fill in the blanks.

(1) (　　　　) (　　　　) (　　　　) to this concert?

(2) This movie (　　　　) (　　　　) social reform.

(3) A few minutes' walk (　　　　) (　　　　) (　　　　) (　　　　) the theater.

(4) (　　　　) you (　　　　) (　　　　) the news?

(5) (　　　　) (　　　　) you (　　　　) going to the show yesterday?

Part 3 50

Listen to some short conversations. You will hear and read two questions about each conversation. Choose the best answer to each question.

[1] Questions (1) and (2) refer to the following conversation.

(1) Where are they going to go?
(A) A laboratory. (B) A museum. (C) A library. (D) A theater.

(2) What kind of movie are they going to watch?
(A) Science fiction. (B) Documentary. (C) Adventure. (D) Comedy.

[2] Questions (3) and (4) refer to the following conversation.

(3) What did the man buy?
(A) An electric keyboard. (B) A vintage book.
(C) An electric book. (D) A right to download.

(4) What does the woman say about the e-book?
(A) It's thick. (B) It's expensive. (C) It's close. (D) It's light.

Don't sweat the small stuff. [proverb]

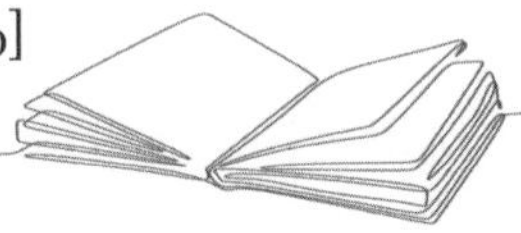

Part 4 51

Listen to some short talks. You will hear and read two questions about each talk. Choose the best answer to each question.

[1] Questions (1) and (2) refer to the following announcement.

(1) What is suggested about the club members?
(A) They have never met before.
(B) There are no new members.
(C) There is one old member.
(D) There are some new members.

(2) What will the members most likely do when the meeting ends?
(A) Write a report.
(B) Buy a new book.
(C) Make a book suggestion.
(D) Make a cup of tea.

[2] Questions (3) and (4) refer to the following talk.

(3) What is the speaker giving advice about?
(A) How to learn a language.
(B) How to find new things.
(C) How to pass exams.
(D) How to write well.

(4) What does the speaker say is important?
(A) To increase study time.
(B) To read interesting articles.
(C) To write something exciting.
(D) To study hard.

Reading Section Practice

Part 1

Each sentence has a space where a word or phrase is missing. Choose the best answer to complete the sentence.

(1) The movie made __________ so happy.
(A) I (B) me (C) our (D) his

(2) The rain __________ us indoors watching TV all day.
(A) soaked (B) looked (C) fell (D) kept

(3) Her discovery __________ her wealth and fame.
(A) sought (B) caught (C) fought (D) brought

(4) The hurricane __________ us from going to the concert.
(A) prevailed (B) prevented (C) promoted (D) pretended

(5) This movie __________ me a new outlook on life.
(A) gave (B) stopped (C) took (D) dug

(6) The song __________ me of my childhood.
(A) takes (B) remembers (C) reminds (D) knows

(7) The last scene of the drama __________ me uneasy.
(A) saw (B) arrived (C) departed (D) left

(8) This new device __________ us to watch movies anywhere we like.
(A) enlarges (B) enables (C) enriches (D) encounters

Part 2

Each of the short texts has three spaces where a word or phrase is missing. For each space, choose the best answer to complete the text.

[1] Questions (1) to (3) refer to the following article.

Utilize your nearby library with your e-books

Did you know that most local libraries and schools now [(1)] their own catalogue of e-books. For public libraries, you need a library card and PIN number to download books [(2)] your device. For school libraries, you will need your student number and PIN number to log-in to the system and borrow materials.

After the borrowing period is up, library e-books are automatically returned. This will [(3)] you time so that you can spend more time reading!

(1) (A) are	(B) read	(C) listen	(D) have
(2) (A) to	(B) from	(C) off	(D) of
(3) (A) take	(B) save	(C) note	(D) examine

[2] Questions (4) to (6) refer to the following advertisement.

"SMART E-WATCH"

Our newly [(4)] wristwatch "Smart E-Watch" is a smartwatch that connects to your smartphone, which [(5)] you to make calls, send texts and run applications. There are many more things Smart-E Watch can do for you.

We added new watch faces, health care and cycle tracking. This is not the only watch that connects to most popular smartphones, but it really [(6)] a lot of users. You can also record a voice memo, connect to your car, check email, and share your location.

(4) (A) design	(B) designed	(C) designing	(D) designer
(5) (A) able	(B) enables	(C) enabling	(D) abilities
(6) (A) interest	(B) interests	(C) interested	(D) interesting

Part 3

Texts such as notices, letters and instant messages are followed by two or three questions. Choose the best answer to each question.

[1] Questions (1) and (2) refer to the following notice.

Hillwood Library

Opening times	*Services at the Library*
Monday: 12 P.M. to 7 P.M.	• Books for loan
Tuesday - Friday: 10 A.M. to 7 P.M.	• Newspapers and Magazines
Saturday: 10 A.M. to 5 P.M.	• Use a library computer or access free Wi-Fi
Sunday: Closed	• Printing and Scanning services

(1) What day does the library close early?
(A) Sunday (B) Monday (C) Wednesday (D) Saturday

(2) Which service is NOT available?
(A) Borrowing books (B) Using the internet
(C) Printing files (D) Photocopying documents

[2] Questions (3) and (4) refer to the following text message.

Rosie: Hi. Have you finished your biology homework yet?

James: Yes, I just finished. It was very interesting.

Rosie: Really? I haven't started. I lost my textbook. Can I borrow yours?

James: ______________________________

(3) What does Rosie want James to do?
(A) Finish his homework (B) Help her with her homework
(C) Help her find her textbook (D) Lend her a textbook

(4) Select the best response to Rosie's message.
(A) "Sure, I'll bring it to school tomorrow."
(B) "I haven't finished my homework yet."
(C) "Sure, you can give it to me tomorrow."
(D) "No, it was really interesting."

Stage 2

Unit 11 Online Friends

Grammar Target: Reported Speech

Vocabulary Check 52

Listen to the following sentences and fill in the blanks.

(a) They (　　　　　) (　　　　　) together.
(b) (　　　　　) (　　　　　) (　　　　　) take a break?
(c) I learned it (　　　　　) (　　　　　) (　　　　　).
(d) I have (　　　　　) (　　　　　) (　　　　　) coming tonight.
(e) Please (　　　　　) your (　　　　　) (　　　　　) (　　　　　).
(f) It's (　　　　　) (　　　　　) (　　　　　) (　　　　　) photos in here.

Listening Section Practice

Part 1 53

[1] Choose the picture that the phrase or sentence best describes.

(A)

(B)

(C)

(D)

[2] Listen again to the sentence and fill in the blanks.

Women are (　　　　　) (　　　　　) (　　　　　).

Part 2 54

[1] Listen to questions or statements. After each question or statement, you will hear and read four responses. Choose the best response.

(1) (A) Yes, it's hard. (B) No, I don't. (C) Yes, he did. (D) No, he won't.
(2) (A) Oh, you like it. (B) If you say so.
(C) I love shopping. (D) Yes, I did.
(3) (A) I had fun in the class. (B) It seems nice.
(C) The manager called me. (D) I cancel it.
(4) (A) Yes, she did. (B) It's the right date.
(C) I'd say yes, of course. (D) She has the data.
(5) (A) I had lunch. (B) Come together. (C) Dinner's ready. (D) Yes, let's.

[2] Listen again to each question or statement and fill in the blanks.

(1) I (　　　　) Mr. Harrison (　　　　) to (　　　　) (　　　　).
(2) (　　　　) you (　　　　) you (　　　　) that store?
(3) (　　　　) (　　　　) you the computer class (　　　　) (　　　　) today?
(4) (　　　　) (　　　　) you (　　　　) if she (　　　　) you on a date?
(5) (　　　　) (　　　　) (　　　　) (　　　　) go for dinner together?

Part 3 55

Listen to some short conversations. You will hear and read two questions about each conversation. Choose the best answer to each question.

[1] Questions (1) and (2) refer to the following conversation.

(1) What does the man think about love online?
(A) Unnatural. (B) Very popular. (C) So interesting. (D) Not usual.

(2) Where did the woman meet her boyfriend?
(A) At school. (B) In an office. (C) Online. (D) At a party.

[2] Questions (3) and (4) refer to the following conversation.

(3) How does the man look?
(A) Nervous. (B) Embarrassed. (C) Confused. (D) Excited.

(4) What is the man waiting for?
(A) A phone call. (B) Lunch. (C) Dinner. (D) A reply.

Strategies for TOEIC BRIDGE #5

Listening Part 3 – Conversations

In this section you will listen to short conversations. Try to read the questions and answer choices before listening to the dialogue. It will help prepare your mind to imagine the situation and identify the correct answer more easily.

Try to determine the relationship of the speakers. Are they friends, family, co-workers, teacher and student, or doctor and patient? This will help you

Part 4 56

Listen to some short talks. You will hear and read two questions about each talk. Choose the best answer to each question.

[1] Questions (1) and (2) refer to the following telephone message.

(1) Why is the woman not able to meet Dave?
(A) She has to visit a client. (B) She was late for work.
(C) She didn't ask her boss. (D) She has a meeting.

(2) What will the woman do when she finishes work?
(A) Write up a report. (B) Make a call.
(C) Talk to her boss. (D) Make dinner.

[2] Questions (3) and (4) refer to the following announcement.

(3) Who are the listeners?
(A) Teachers. (B) Office workers. (C) Students. (D) Customers.

(4) What should the listeners do with their phones?
(A) Turn off the sound. (B) Keep their phone in their bags.
(C) Take photos. (D) Check their email.

Reading Section Practice

Part 1

Each sentence has a space where a word or phrase is missing. Choose the best answer to complete the sentence.

(1) She said she __________ come to the party.
(A) will (B) would (C) can (D) may

(2) Paul always asks me when I __________ available for dinner.
(A) be (B) am (C) will be (D) would be

(3) Did you tell them that you __________ London this summer?
(A) would come (B) can go (C) will be (D) would visit

(4) I said to her " __________ see that movie."
(A) go (B) going (C) to go (D) went

(5) They demanded George __________ the chairperson.
(A) be (B) is (C) will be (D) was

(6) She asked me " __________ you online?"
(A) is (B) are (C) to be (D) being

(7) We asked him how he __________ his wife.
(A) meet (B) meets (C) will meet (D) met

(8) John asked Yoko __________ his team.
(A) join (B) joined (C) will join (D) to join

Part 2

Each of the short texts has three spaces where a word or phrase is missing. For each space, choose the best answer to complete the text.

[1] Questions (1) to (3) refer to the following article.

5 Ways for Children to Use the Internet Safely

In modern society, children are almost always [(1)]. They can access information online in many ways. And yet online access comes with risks. To keep children safe, tell them [(2)] the following when they are online.

1. Use the privacy settings.
2. Think [(3)] you post.
3. Speak up if you see someone bullied.
4. Ask for permission before you meet online friends.
5. Keep adults in the loop.

(1) (A) connect (B) connects (C) connected (D) connecting
(2) (A) do (B) to do (C) doing (D) would do
(3) (A) before (B) after (C) above (D) below

[2] Questions (4) to (6) refer to the following article.

Online Conferencing

The main purpose of online conferencing is to [(4)] face-to-face communication between two or more people in different locations. It is a popular alternative to phone conferencing for businesses. It provides individual users with an inexpensive [(5)] of communication with distant friends and family.

The face-to-face communication through the Internet helps business contacts to create a sense of community, even between people who have never [(6)] met.

(4) (A) enlarge (B) engage (C) endure (D) enable
(5) (A) mean (B) means (C) meaning (D) meant
(6) (A) mentally (B) socially (C) ironically (D) physically

Part 3

Texts such as notices, letters and instant messages are followed by two or three questions. Choose the best answer to each question.

[1] Questions (1) and (2) refer to the following article.

Schools complain that children spend more time on their smartphones than on school work. This is a worrying trend. A recent survey shows that on average 10-year-olds spend at least 2 hours a day on their phones. 12 to 13 year-olds spend an average of 3 hours, while 14 to 16 year-olds spend as much at 6 hours a day. With cases of online bullying increasing, it is important for children to have time away from phones and to spend time with friends in real life. Many say that parents need to make stricter rules about phone usage.

(1) What is the article about?
(A) Smartphones can help children with homework.
(B) Children use smartphones in class to study.
(C) Smartphones are not used by children.
(D) Children spend too much time on smartphones.

(2) Who uses smartphones for the longest time?
(A) Ten-year-olds (B) Twelve-year-olds
(C) Sixteen-year-olds (D) Parents

[2] Questions (3) and (4) refer to the following online chat conversation.

Kate [8:45 P.M.]: Do you realize we've been friends for nearly a year now?

Ben [8:48 P.M.]: Really? It seems like only yesterday we started chatting in the Worldwide Book Club.

Kate [8:52 P.M.]: Maybe it's time we meet up?

Ben [8:54 P.M.]: I think that's a great idea. Where shall we meet?

Kate [9:01 P.M.]: I'll look up a restaurant that is halfway between where we live, we can meet after work. What do you think?

Ben [9:04 P.M.]: Sounds great. Let me know where.

(3) What is suggested about Ben and Kate?
(A) They have just met online. (B) They have never met in real life.
(C) They haven't met for a long time. (D) They both work in a book shop.

(4) What most likely will Kate do next?
(A) Go to meet Ben (B) Check the book club forum
(C) Go to work (D) Find a restaurant

Unit 12 Productivity

Grammar Target: Adjectives and Adverbs

Vocabulary Check 57

Listen to the following sentences and fill in the blanks.

(a) Can you (   ) a (   ) (   ) at the paper?

(b) He is a (   ) (   ) scholar.

(c) The new (   ) is (   ) (   ).

(d) (   ) did you (   ) in the office (   )?

(e) (   ) is not a (   ) (   ) way to work.

(f) I will (   ) her (   ).

Listening Section Practice

Part 1 58

[1] Choose the picture that the phrase or sentence best describes.

(A)

(B)

(C)

(D)

[2] Listen again to the sentence and fill in the blanks.

Documents are (   ) (   ) on the desk.

Part 2 59

[1] Listen to questions or statements. After each question or statement, you will hear and read four responses. Choose the best response.

(1) (A) It goes so quickly. (B) You could do that.
(C) Yes, I looked for it. (D) Sure, no problem.

(2) (A) It's a short walk. (B) No, her office is closed.
(C) Ok, I can wait. (D) Yes, it's back.

(3) (A) He got a new one. (B) There's no hope for success.
(C) I'm at work. (D) Good for you!

(4) (A) Sorry I'm late. (B) He's been on a business trip.
(C) I like the scenery. (D) No, he doesn't.

(5) (A) I liked the present. (B) Six attended.
(C) They were nice. (D) I often meet her.

[2] Listen again to each question or statement and fill in the blanks.

(1) Could you (　　　　) a (　　　　) (　　　　) at this paper?
(2) I'll be (　　　　) in the office (　　　　).
(3) I (　　　　) (　　　　) (　　　　) getting a new job.
(4) (　　　　) you (　　　　) Mr. Johnson in the office (　　　　)?
(5) (　　　　) (　　　　) people were (　　　　) at the meeting?

Part 3 60

Listen to some short conversations. You will hear and read two questions about each conversation. Choose the best answer to each question.

[1] Questions (1) and (2) refer to the following conversation.

(1) Who is Mr. Emerson?
(A) A colleague. (B) An examinee. (C) A new boss. (D) A friend.

(2) What is the woman going to do tomorrow?
(A) Go to a party. (B) See her friend. (C) Stay in the office. (D) Meet her client.

[2] Questions (3) and (4) refer to the following conversation.

(3) How does the woman look?
(A) Tired. (B) Worried. (C) Nervous. (D) Sad.

(4) Where is the woman going to go tonight?
(A) A seminar. (B) The airport.
(C) A project meeting. (D) Dinner.

Every cloud has a silver lining. [proverb]

Part 4 61

Listen to some short talks. You will hear and read two questions about each talk. Choose the best answer to each question.

[1] Questions (1) and (2) refer to the following talk.

(1) What is the advice for?
(A) How to multitask.
(B) How to work more quickly.
(C) How to take notes.
(D) How to increase your workload.

(2) What happens when you multitask?
(A) You get more done.
(B) You have more energy.
(C) Your brain function improves.
(D) You work more slowly.

[2] Questions (3) and (4) refer to the following telephone message.

(3) Why is the woman going to be late?
(A) She has a meeting.
(B) She worked for 30 minutes.
(C) She forgot her schedule.
(D) The train is late.

(4) What will Dave most likely do next?
(A) Cancel the meetings.
(B) Make a reservation for lunch.
(C) Check the train times.
(D) Call the clients.

Reading Section Practice

Part 1

Each sentence has a space where a word or phrase is missing. Choose the best answer to complete the sentence.

(1) They examined the new product very __________ .
(A) care (B) careful (C) carefully (D) carefulness

(2) What does it take to become a __________ learner?
(A) success (B) succeed (C) successful (D) successfully

(3) She always does her assignments so __________.
(A) effecting (B) efficiency (C) efficient (D) efficiently

(4) President Johnson is __________ in himself.
(A) confidence (B) confident (C) confidently (D) confidential

(5) Lucy came up with a very __________ idea.
(A) produce (B) product (C) productivity (D) productive

(6) All employees must attend the meeting __________ after the lunch break.
(A) short (B) shortly (C) shorten (D) shortened

(7) Paul's office is so __________ that he can hardly concentrate on his work.
(A) mess (B) messy (C) mass (D) massive

(8) The speaker on the stage should speak __________ enough to be heard.
(A) loud (B) loudly (C) aloud (D) louden

Part 2

Each of the short texts has three spaces where a word or phrase is missing. For each space, choose the best answer to complete the text.

[1] Questions (1) to (3) refer to the following e-mail.

To:	All employees
Subject:	RECYCLING CONTAINERS

I noticed that it has become very [(1)] to keep the supply room neat and tidy.

Please note that it is the duty of all staff members to keep the supply room clean and [(2)]. So, I would like to request you all that when you use the supply room, please make sure that you leave it in the [(3)] condition as you found it.

Thank you for your cooperation.

(1) (A) hard	(B) harden	(C) hardly	(D) hardness
(2) (A) order	(B) orderly	(C) ordered	(D) ordering
(3) (A) beauty	(B) cleaning	(C) different	(D) same

[2] Questions (4) to (6) refer to the following article.

Tips on how to prioritize and organize your work

Time management is [(4)] in getting your work done. It is also important to prioritize, organize, and plan your work. You need to identify which things need to be done [(5)]. It is a crucial process, but once you get used to it, organizing and planning will become easy. If you know how to effectively organize and prioritize your workload, you will learn how to be more efficient and productive.

Try the following tips.

1. Make your to-do list.
2. Rank your to-do list.
3. Post your to-do list.
4. Avoid [(6)] tasks.
5. Set realistic deadlines.

(4) (A) essence	(B) essential	(C) essentially	(D) essentiality
(5) (A) start	(B) top	(C) up	(D) first
(6) (A) necessity	(B) need	(C) needing	(D) unnecessary

Part 3

Texts such as notices, letters and instant messages are followed by two or three questions. Choose the best answer to each question.

[1] Questions (1) and (2) refer to the following memo.

To:	All employees
Subject:	New Flexi Time Guidelines

With regard to the result of the survey last month about working styles, we have decided to introduce a new flexi time policy. There will now be three possible start times for the sales department. Please speak to your supervisors to arrange the schedules. Non-sales team will also have the option to work from home once or twice a week. Hours worked will be logged on the new computer systems. If you have any questions, please speak to Charlotte in personnel.

(1) What was the reason for the change in work times?
(A) Results of a questionnaire.
(B) A change in computer systems.
(C) Supervisors need a new schedule.
(D) The company needs to save money.

(2) Who is NOT able to work from home?
(A) Personnel staff
(B) Sales staff
(C) Managers
(D) Office staff

[2] Questions (3) and (4) refer to the following text message.

Craig: Hi. I have to finish the yearly sales report by tomorrow and can't get into the office for the meeting. Could you get the meeting notes and forward them to me?

John: Sure, no problem. I hope you get it finished quickly.

(3) Why is Craig unable to attend the meeting?
(A) His car is broken.
(B) He has another meeting.
(C) He needs make more sales.
(D) He hasn't finished his work.

(4) What will John do after the meeting?
(A) Call Craig
(B) E-mail Craig
(C) Leave the office
(D) Make a report

Unit 13 Pets

Grammar Target: Prepositions of Place

Vocabulary Check 62

Listen to the following sentences and fill in the blanks.

(a) My dog is (　　　　　) (　　　　　) the (　　　　　).

(b) I (　　　　　) my cats (　　　　　) (　　　　　) (　　　　　).

(c) I (　　　　　) my cat to the (　　　　　).

(d) Do you know (　　　　　) to (　　　　　) (　　　　　) rabbits?

(e) I (　　　　　) an (　　　　　) (　　　　　) the (　　　　　).

(f) The dog is (　　　　　) the (　　　　　).

Listening Section Practice

Part 1 63

[1] Choose the picture that the phrase or sentence best describes.

(A)

(B)

(C)

(D)

[2] Listen again to the sentence and fill in the blanks.

A boy (　　　　　) (　　　　　) his dog (　　　　　) the river.

Part 2 64

[1] Listen to questions or statements. After each question or statement, you will hear and read four responses. Choose the best response.

(1) (A) It's mine. (B) It's by the fireplace.
(C) She's fine. (D) I'm from Tokyo.

(2) (A) I'm not lying. (B) You have a dog.
(C) Yes, it's cute. (D) Keep off the grass, please.

(3) (A) I picked it up for you. (B) Are you leaving?
(C) To the left. (D) It's tied to it.

(4) (A) Last time I saw it. (B) I see it twice a week.
(C) I've never had a cat. (D) I saw it in the backyard.

(5) (A) Yes, I already took my cat there. (B) Pets are not allowed in here.
(C) No, I can't take my pet on the train. (D) Yes, she lives near the station.

[2] Listen again to each question or statement and fill in the blanks.

(1) (   ) (   ) your (   )?
(2) (   ) you (   ) the dog (   ) (   ) the grass?
(3) I (   ) my dog's leash (   ) the (   ).
(4) (   ) did you (   ) my cat (   )?
(5) (   ) you (   ) (   ) the grand opening of the pet salon (   ) the station?

Part 3 65

Listen to some short conversations. You will hear and read two questions about each conversation. Choose the best answer to each question.

[1] Questions (1) and (2) refer to the following conversation.

(1) Where was the man in the morning?
(A) In the city hall. (B) In his house. (C) In a gym. (D) In the park.

(2) How is the man?
(A) Sleepy. (B) Nervous. (C) Exhausted. (D) Healthy.

[2] Questions (3) and (4) refer to the following conversation.

(3) What happened to the woman's dog?
(A) It got sick. (B) It lost its tooth. (C) It ate too much. (D) It broke its leg.

(4) Where is the woman going to go tomorrow?
(A) The office. (B) The kitchen. (C) The animal clinic. (D) The food store.

Part 4 66

Listen to some short talks. You will hear and read two questions about each talk. Choose the best answer to each question.

[1] Questions (1) and (2) refer to the following talk.

(1) What does Tom do?
(A) He is a doctor.
(B) He is a vet.
(C) He is a zoo keeper.
(D) He is a teacher.

(2) What advice was NOT given in the talk?
(A) Rabbits need to keep warm.
(B) Rabbits need company.
(C) Rabbits need something to do.
(D) Rabbits need to run.

[2] Questions (3) and (4) refer to the following telephone message.

(3) Where did the caller find the cat?
(A) On the fence.
(B) In the kitchen.
(C) Under the shed.
(D) In the shed.

(4) What will the cat owner most likely do next?
(A) Feed the cat fish.
(C) Collect the cat in the morning.
(C) Keep the cat in the kitchen.
(D) Collect the cat in the afternoon.

Reading Section Practice

Part 1

Each sentence has a space where a word or phrase is missing. Choose the best answer to complete the sentence.

(1) Can you see the birds perched __________ a row?
(A) in (B) from (C) on (D) by

(2) Little birds are waiting to be fed __________ the nest.
(A) afar (B) closely (C) for (D) in

(3) My cat likes to sleep __________ my kids.
(A) besides (B) close (C) among (D) with

(4) My dog always walks __________ me.
(A) of (B) across (C) next to (D) forward

(5) Your cat suddenly hid __________ the table.
(A) below (B) under (C) above (D) onto

(6) A kitten came __________ to its mother when a dog barked.
(A) close (B) together (C) by (D) fast

(7) John told his dog to stay __________ him.
(A) along (B) below (C) of (D) beside

(8) My dog likes sitting __________ us.
(A) over (B) above (C) between (D) off

Part 2

Each of the short texts has three spaces where a word or phrase is missing. For each space, choose the best answer to complete the text.

[1] Questions (1) to (3) refer to the following instruction.

Notice to Pet Owners from Monte Rosa Hotel

Please follow these rules when you come to our hotel with your pets.

1. Your dog must be kept on a leash.

2. You must pick up your dog's waste [(1)] the hotel grounds.

3. You can walk your dog along the road [(2)] the hotel.

We love pets, too. However, pets are not permitted on any furniture, including sofas. If we find that a pet has been [(3)] any of the furniture, we will charge a $50 cleaning fee. We thank you for your cooperation.

(1) (A) out (B) above (C) onto (D) in
(2) (A) behind (B) over (C) with (D) between
(3) (A) below (B) from (C) under (D) on

[2] Questions (4) to (6) refer to the following article.

To the Pet Owners in this Apartment
Please control your dogs' barking!

Dog's barking is one of the most irritating issues for apartment residents. This tends to occur when they hear someone walking [(4)] the hallway or when someone knocks [(5)] the door. It often happens when the owner is out because the dog is scared or sad.

If you have received complaints about the noise from your neighbors, please take it seriously. It may be necessary to consult a dog trainer or a vet on how to control the barking when you're [(6)] home.

(4) (A) behind (B) in (C) besides (D) between
(5) (A) on (B) for (C) of (D) with
(6) (A) close to (B) across from (C) next to (D) away from

Part 3

Texts such as notices, letters and instant messages are followed by two or three questions. Choose the best answer to each question.

[1] Questions (1) and (2) refer to the following postcard.

Dear Sarah,

We are having a great time here in Spain. The weather has been wonderful. The hotel is great. It is by the sea next to a camp site. Many people have their dogs with them. Next time we will stay in a tent so we can bring Billy with us.

Thank you so much for looking after Billy while we are away. Please make sure he stays in the kitchen. He sometimes eats the post! I hope you are enjoying walks with him. We miss him so much.

See you soon!

Christie

(1) Where is Christie staying?
- (A) At a friend's house
- (B) In a caravan
- (C) In a tent
- (D) In a hotel

(2) What is Sarah doing for Christie?
- (A) Taking care of her son
- (B) Watering the plants
- (C) Walking her dog
- (D) Collecting the post

[2] Questions (3) and (4) refer to the following text message.

Joan: Hi. I had to leave early today. I forgot to tell you last night. I didn't want to wake you up. I didn't have time to feed the cat. Could you do it before you go to work?

Mike: ______________________________

(3) What was Mike doing when Joan left the house?
- (A) Feeding the cat
- (B) Working
- (C) Talking on the phone
- (D) Sleeping

(4) Select the best response to Joan's message.
- (A) "Sure, I can. Don't worry."
- (B) "Yes, I remember."
- (C) "Sure, I have a meeting, too."
- (D) "No, I didn't wake up."

Unit 14 Made by Hand

Grammar Target: Passive Voice

Vocabulary Check 67

Listen to the following sentences and fill in the blanks.

(a) He is a very ( ) ( ).

(b) My earrings ( ) ( ) ( ).

(c) My hobbies ( ) ( ).

(d) Good ( ) clothes ( ) ( ) longer.

(e) They ( ) the ( ).

(f) ( ), all items are ( ) ( ).

Listening Section Practice

Part 1 68

[1] Choose the picture that the phrase or sentence best describes.

(A)

(B)

(C)

(D)

[2] Listen again to the sentence and fill in the blanks.

A woman ( ) ( ).

Part 2 69

[1] Listen to questions or statements. After each question or statement, you will hear and read four responses. Choose the best response.

(1) (A) It was made yesterday. (B) I need it.
(C) Another one, please. (D) I did.

(2) (A) I'll do the dishes. (B) How old are you?
(C) You made it. (D) It must be expensive.

(3) (A) Yes, it's all mine. (B) No, I don't.
(C) Yes, I repaired it myself. (D) It's been a year.

(4) (A) Yes, she loves painting. (B) You're talented.
(C) By next month. (D) It's by the door.

(5) (A) No question about it. (B) It's the best year ever.
(C) Yes, it's his selection. (D) He's an electrician.

[2] Listen again to each question or statement and fill in the blanks.

(1) (　　　　) (　　　　) this cake?
(2) This dish (　　　　) (　　　　) four hundred years (　　　　).
(3) (　　　　) your necklace (　　　　) (　　　　)?
(4) (　　　　) this picture really (　　　　) (　　　　) your (　　　　)?
(5) Barry (　　　　) (　　　　) (　　　　) as best artisan this year.

Part 3 70

Listen to some short conversations. You will hear and read two questions about each conversation. Choose the best answer to each question.

[1] Questions (1) and (2) refer to the following conversation.

(1) What does the man want?
(A) A pair of pants. (B) A shirt. (C) A bag. (D) A sewing kit.

(2) How long did it take the woman to make the shirt?
(A) 1 day. (B) 7 days. (C) 10 days. (D) 14 days.

[2] Questions (3) and (4) refer to the following conversation and list.

Handmade Accessories

Ring	one for $5	two for $8
Bracelet	one for $6	two for $10
Earrings	one pair for $8	two pairs for $15
Necklace	one for $8	two for $15

Further discounts on multiple purchases!

(3) What does the man plan to buy?
(A) A bracelet. (B) Earrings. (C) A necklace. (D) A ring.

(4) What color earrings does the woman recommend?
(A) Blue. (B) Pink. (C) Green. (D) Red.

Part 4 71

Listen to some short talks. You will hear and read two questions about each talk. Choose the best answer to each question.

[1] Questions (1) and (2) refer to the following talk.

(1) Why are synthetic fabrics bad for the environment?
(A) They pollute the air.
(B) They are difficult to make.
(C) They pollute the water.
(D) They are expensive.

(2) What kind of clothes should we buy?
(A) Clothes made from polyester.
(B) Cheap clothes.
(C) Second hand clothes.
(D) Designer clothes.

[2] Questions (3) and (4) refer to the following telephone message.

(3) What is sold out?
(A) Cotton t-shirts.
(B) Cotton leggings.
(C) Small beach dresses.
(D) Extra-large beach dresses.

(4) What will Becky do after this call?
(A) Send the order.
(B) Send a catalogue.
(C) E-mail the order.
(D) Give a 10% discount.

Reading Section Practice

Part 1

Each sentence has a space where a word or phrase is missing. Choose the best answer to complete the sentence.

(1) This book cover __________ made by my mother.
(A) was (B) are (C) has (D) does

(2) The vases __________ been fired in the oven overnight.
(A) is (B) are (C) has (D) have

(3) The wine from our winery is made __________ special grapes grown here.
(A) by (B) for (C) of (D) from

(4) All tables put in this shelter are made __________ cardboard.
(A) by (B) of (C) for (D) in

(5) Safety goggles must be __________ when you are in the jewelry factory.
(A) wear (B) wore (C) worn (D) wearing

(6) My favorite fountain pen is now being __________ by the craftsman.
(A) repair (B) repairs (C) repaired (D) repairing

(7) Your order has been __________ from our studio.
(A) discontinued (B) disrespected (C) dismissed (D) dispatched

(8) Who __________ the wall painted by?
(A) do (B) does (C) was (D) has

Part 2

Each of the short texts has three spaces where a word or phrase is missing. For each space, choose the best answer to complete the text.

[1] Questions (1) to (3) refer to the following note.

FAQs on account

▶ *Why do I need an account?*

Creating an account with Handmade-Clothing.com assists you by saving delivery details and your orders so that they can be easily tracked [(1)] you.

▶ *What happens if I forget my password?*

An email will be [(2)] to your account email address with your password information. You can then reset your password.

▶ *Is my personal data safe if I create an account?*

Yes. Only your delivery details [(3)] saved. No credit card information is saved.

(1) (A) with	(B) over	(C) by	(D) from
(2) (A) placed	(B) bought	(C) canceled	(D) sent
(3) (A) is	(B) are	(C) have	(D) has

[2] Questions (4) to (6) refer to the following article.

Introduction to Making Handmade Paper

Paper is one of the most common commodities in daily life, but making paper at home is not so popular. Actually very few people [(4)] taught how to make paper, and they are not familiar with the techniques involved.

I would like to show you how paper is [(5)]. You probably already have most of the equipment in your house. Making paper is not only for fun [(6)] will also help us to become more aware of the value of paper. In this way we can help reduce waste in our society.

(4) (A) do	(B) make	(C) is	(D) are
(5) (A) made	(B) pointed	(C) torn	(D) worn
(6) (A) however	(B) without	(C) although	(D) but

Reality is something you rise above.

[Lisa Minnelli]

Part 3

Texts such as notices, letters and instant messages are followed by two or three questions. Choose the best answer to each question.

[1] Questions (1) and (2) refer to the following notice.

Please note that all our clothes are made from natural fibers. We only stock wool, cotton, and bamboo. We believe this is a small step towards a more sustainable future. The clothes are dyed with vegetable dyes to avoid chemicals. So there may be some variation in colors. All items are handmade. They were made in small workshops in good working conditions for a fair wage. Every little bit helps to make the world a better place.

(1) Why may there be some differences in colors?
(A) Because chemicals were used.
(B) Because they are handmade.
(C) Because vegetable dyes were used.
(D) Because they are sustainable.

(2) What is suggested about the clothes?
(A) They are made from synthetic fabrics.
(B) They are made by hand.
(C) They are cheap.
(D) They are mass produced.

[2] Questions (3) and (4) refer to the following web page notice.

New Range of Eco-fashion for Summer!

We are pleased to introduce our new line of business wear. Say goodbye to hot sweaty synthetic suits and hello to cool bamboo fabric. Due to a new weaving technique we have created a fabric which is both durable and cool. Due to the popularity of these suits we have sold out of extra-large sized. But a new shipment is expected soon. Customers who pre-order the extra-large size will receive a 10% discount.

Orders received before 12 P.M. will be sent the same day.

(3) What is suggested about the new product?
(A) It is for casual wear.
(B) It uses a new fabric.
(C) It uses polyester fabric.
(D) It is not selling well.

(4) What do we know about bamboo fabric?
(A) It is 10% cheaper.
(B) It is synthetic.
(C) It is very warm.
(D) It is cool to wear.

Strategies for TOEIC BRIDGE #6

Reading Part 3 – Reading Comprehension

Try to approach this task as an "information finding" activity rather than focusing on the difficulty of the text.

First, read through the text quickly for a general idea of the purpose. Don't worry about words you don't understand. To guess the meaning of words in context is also an important reading skill. Then, read the questions and return to the text to find the answers.

Unit 15 Writing

Grammar Target: Conjunctions

Vocabulary Check 72

Listen to the following sentences and fill in the blanks.

(a) There (   ) (   ) a make-up (   ).
(b) Don't (   ) (   ) (   ) your portfolio.
(c) She (   ) (   ) literature.
(d) We will (   ) (   ) useful (   ).
(e) Please (   ) your (   ).
(f) (   ) you (   ) to (   ) for this job?

Listening Section Practice

Part 1 73

[1] Choose the picture that the phrase or sentence best describes.

(A)

(B)

(C)

(D)

[2] Listen again to the sentence and fill in the blanks.

A man in a suit (   ) a (   ) of (   ).

Part 2 74

[1] Listen to questions or statements. After each question or statement, you will hear and read four responses. Choose the best response.

(1) (A) Oh, thank you. (B) You're welcome.
(C) Yes, I did. (D) No, it's not in here.

(2) (A) It's been hot these days. (B) I'll see you tomorrow.
(C) The line is busy right now. (D) It's due next week.

(3) (A) To the left. (B) I often see him.
(C) Thanks for your help. (D) I don't have classes.

(4) (A) She had written a letter. (B) I hope he does well.
(C) He was having fun. (D) He is with me.

(5) (A) I am the leader. (B) I read it yesterday.
(C) Did you write it? (D) But you need these skills.

[2] Listen again to each question or statement and fill in the blanks.

(1) Excuse me. (　　　　　) this (　　　　　) (　　　　　)?
(2) I haven't (　　　　　) my resume (　　　　　) I've been busy.
(3) (　　　　　) straight (　　　　　) you'll (　　　　　) the school on your left.
(4) John is (　　　　　) (　　　　　) he (　　　　　) a writing test.
(5) I don't like reading, (　　　　　) (　　　　　) (　　　　　) like writing.

Part 3 75

Listen to some short conversations. You will hear and read two questions about each conversation. Choose the best answer to each question.

[1] Questions (1) and (2) refer to the following conversation.

(1) What does the man say about the writing test?
(A) Easy. (B) Difficult. (C) Same as usual. (D) Unexpected.

(2) What is the woman going to do?
(A) Put on make-up. (B) Help the man. (C) Write a letter. (D) Take a test.

[2] Questions (3) and (4) refer to the following conversation.

(3) When is the deadline of the paper?
(A) Yesterday. (B) Tomorrow. (C) A week later. (D) Next month.

(4) What was the woman's major when she was in college?
(A) Literature. (B) History. (C) Science. (D) German.

Part 4 76

Listen to some short talks. You will hear and read two questions about each talk. Choose the best answer to each question.

[1] Questions (1) and (2) refer to the following announcement.

(1) What is the course for?
- (A) To learn different styles of communication.
- (B) To learn about business meetings.
- (C) To learn how to study effectively.
- (D) To learn how to write business letters.

(2) What will the students need to do every week?
- (A) Go to a meeting.
- (B) Think of new expressions.
- (C) Write a letter.
- (D) Mark an assignment.

[2] Questions (3) and (4) refer to the following talk.

(3) Who is the advice for?
- (A) Someone who wants a new job.
- (B) Someone who is starting university.
- (C) Someone who wants to get a qualification.
- (D) Someone who wants to be a writer.

(4) Which of the following suggestions was NOT mentioned in the talk?
- (A) Write about your interests.
- (B) Write about what you can do for the company.
- (C) Tell them why you are writing.
- (D) Don't write a long email.

Reading Section Practice

Part 1

Each sentence has a space where a word or phrase is missing. Choose the best answer to complete the sentence.

(1) Lucy wrote a cover letter carefully, __________ she was going to have a job interview.
(A) yet (B) but (C) or (D) as

(2) She was not happy with her writing __________ everyone praised it.
(A) due (B) nor (C) unless (D) but

(3) This job involves __________ writing and reading skills.
(A) both (B) either (C) neither (D) also

(4) I wrote down her address so __________ I wouldn't forget it.
(A) for (B) since (C) well (D) that

(5) The printer ran out of ink __________ I was making some handouts.
(A) if (B) so (C) while (D) that

(6) It has been ten years ________ he started working as a journalist.

(A) for (B) since (C) before (D) when

(7) Harry read the letter again ________ again.

(A) but (B) so (C) or (D) and

(8) Her comments were blunt ________ effective.

(A) as (B) but (C) since (D) unless

Part 2

Each of the short texts has three spaces where a word or phrase is missing. For each space, choose the best answer to complete the text.

[1] Questions (1) to (3) refer to the following article.

Want to be a Journalist?

Journalists write [(1)] assemble news stories. Their job involves reading many kinds of articles, attending events, writing, editing, and proofreading. They try to make their articles clear and interesting. In this way they tell their audience about what's going on in the world.

[(2)] there are several routes to journalism for both university graduates and high school graduates, some companies ask for a university degree. [(3)] any subject is acceptable, English or journalism are preferred. Also, some jobs may require candidates to take extra courses in journalism.

(1) (A) but (B) or (C) nor (D) and

(2) (A) Because (B) Nevertheless (C) Unless (D) Although

(3) (A) While (B) Since (C) Because (D) Though

[2] Questions (4) to (6) refer to the following note.

Keys to successful diary writing for English practice

Writing a diary is easy. There are no special rules you have to follow [(4)] you can simply write whatever comes to your mind as you write. [(5)], you should be honest with yourself when you write. Also stick to the schedule that you have set for yourself and be natural. [(6)] you finish writing your dairy entries, it is nice to go through the entries to find, punctuation, spelling, and grammar mistakes.

(4) (A) but (B) so (C) till (D) unless

(5) (A) While (B) Whereas (C) Before (D) However

(6) (A) Before (B) After (C) Since (D) Although

Part 3

Texts such as notices, letters and instant messages are followed by two or three questions. Choose the best answer to each question.

[1] Questions (1) and (2) refer to the following memo.

To:	All employees
Subject:	Weekend Seminars

Please don't forget to sign up for at least one seminar for the internal company training program this weekend. Some of them are beginning to fill up quickly, so put your name down early to avoid disappointment. There is only one space left on the seminar on how to hold effective meetings, and there are only four spaces left on the business writing course. Time management and coping with stress still have availability.

(1) What will employees be doing this weekend?
- (A) Going on a business trip
- (B) Going away for training
- (C) Attending business lessons
- (D) Learning how to train

(2) Which seminar is most popular?
- (A) Business Writing
- (B) Effective Meetings
- (C) Time Management
- (D) Coping with Stress

[2] Questions (3) and (4) refer to the following notice.

The Art of Writing

A two-day workshop for beginner calligraphy in the beautiful Devon countryside.
Stay in a quiet farmhouse, eating freshly cooked farm produce, while learning from Patricia Doley. Patricia has been practicing calligraphy for over thirty years. She will expertly teach the basic skills and also look into how to keep improving after the course.

(3) Why will people join the course for the weekend?
- (A) To learn how to cook
- (B) To experience farm work
- (C) To learn how to write beautifully
- (D) To walk in the countryside

(4) What is suggested about Patricia?
- (A) She likes eating.
- (B) She is a quiet person.
- (C) She likes farm work.
- (D) She is an experienced calligrapher.

Unit 16 Food Culture

Grammar Target: Relative Pronouns

Vocabulary Check

77

Listen to the following sentences and fill in the blanks.

(a) (   ) you (   ) any musical (   )?

(b) He is (   ) (   ) Chinese.

(c) This is (   ) I (   ) to study (   ).

(d) I am (   ) (   ) foreign languages.

(e) Thank you (   ) (   ).

(f) I (   ) a (   ) for dinner.

Listening Section Practice

Part 1 78

[1] Choose the picture that the phrase or sentence best describes.

(A)

(B)

(C)

(D)

[2] Listen again to the sentence and fill in the blanks.

(   ) (   ) (   ).

Part 2 (Track 79)

[1] Listen to questions or statements. After each question or statement, you will hear and read four responses. Choose the best response.

(1) (A) Whose guitar is this? (B) My sister does.
(C) If you say so. (D) Is she famous?

(2) (A) How are you? (B) You're so clever.
(C) No problem. (D) It's my resolution.

(3) (A) I'm from India. (B) I've never been there.
(C) No, I haven't. (D) Yes, please.

(4) (A) How did you like it? (B) I often visit him.
(C) No, I'm not. (D) Are you from Canada?

(5) (A) I lost my wallet. (B) Where are you from?
(C) It's difficult. (D) Yes, it's crowded everywhere.

[2] Listen again to each question or statement and fill in the blanks.

(1) I have a (   ) (   ) sister (   ) Indian music.
(2) This is (   ) (   ) (   ) the problem.
(3) (   ) you ever (   ) to sitar, (   ) (   ) an Indian musical instrument?
(4) Canada is the (   ) country (   ) I (   ).
(5) New York is a (   ) (   ) you can easily (   ) (   ).

Part 3 (Track 80)

Listen to some short conversations. You will hear and read two questions about each conversation. Choose the best answer to each question.

[1] Questions (1) and (2) refer to the following conversation.

(1) What is the woman interested in?
(A) A workshop. (B) A dance contest.
(C) A vendor. (D) A music concert.

(2) What is the man planning to do?
(A) Eat Malaysian food. (B) Dance all night.
(C) Sell items. (D) Enter a dance competition.

[2] Questions (3) and (4) refer to the following conversation.

(3) How long has the man taken French lessons?
(A) For half a year. (B) Since last year.
(C) For a year. (D) For two years.

(4) What are the woman and the man going to do next?
(A) Study French. (B) Eat French food.
(C) Cook lunch. (D) Visit France.

Part 4 81

Listen to some short talks. You will hear and read two questions about each talk. Choose the best answer to each question.

[1] Questions (1) and (2) refer to the following talk.

(1) Who is speaking?
(A) A stall holder.
(B) A volunteer.
(C) An exchange advisor.
(D) An event organizer.

(2) What can you do at this event?
(A) Learn foreign languages.
(B) Meet foreign singers.
(C) Talk to people from other countries.
(D) Buy tickets to other countries.

[2] Questions (3) and (4) refer to the following telephone message.

(3) What is said about the Indian Restaurant?
(A) It is fully booked.
(B) It is closed for two weeks.
(C) It doesn't take reservations.
(D) It isn't open tonight.

(4) What will Jane do?
(A) Call the Indian restaurant.
(B) Cook spicy food.
(C) Go out for dinner tonight.
(D) Learn how to cook Thai food.

Reading Section Practice

Part 1

Each sentence has a space where a word or phrase is missing. Choose the best answer to complete the sentence.

(1) Mr. Shankar is a musician ________ introduced Indian music to the world.
(A) who (B) where (C) whose (D) which

(2) A bagel is a kind of a round bread ________ was developed in New York.
(A) who (B) which (C) where (D) when

(3) March 17 is the day ________ we celebrate St. Patrick's Day.
(A) who (B) when (C) whom (D) where

(4) I have a friend ________ mother came from Thailand.
(A) who (B) whose (C) which (D) where

(5) Those ________ participated in the event had a lot of fun.
(A) who (B) whose (C) when (D) which

(6) Do you know the reason ________ Mrs. Baker returned to her country?
(A) who (B) which (C) what (D) why

(7) Mr. Perry has the foreign stamp ________ I have been looking.
(A) that (B) in which (C) for which (D) by whom

(8) ________ you learn through the cultural exchange will help you know your country better.
(A) What (B) While (C) Where (D) When

Part 2

Each of the short texts has three spaces where a word or phrase is missing. For each space, choose the best answer to complete the text.

[1] Questions (1) to (3) refer to the following article.

Indian Dish - Naan

Naan is a soft Indian bread [(1)] is traditionally made in a tandoor. The dough gets slapped against the walls of the tandoor, [(2)] it adheres and bakes quickly. You may say no one has a tandoor in the house unless you live in India … That's fine! Believe it or not, it's easy to make your naan at home — [(3)] you need is a non-stick pan!

(1) (A) who	(B) which	(C) where	(D) whose
(2) (A) that	(B) where	(C) whom	(D) if
(3) (A) That	(B) While	(C) Every	(D) All

[2] Questions (4) to (6) refer to the following article.

Koto

The Japanese harp - *koto* is one of a series of Japanese traditional instruments [(4)] give Japanese music its distinctive sound.

Koto was introduced to Japan in the early seventh century from China for the first time. Evolving from its original five-string style to [(5)] is now the basic 13-string instrument, *koto* has become one of the Japan's national instruments. *Koto* measures about 70-inch long. The player usually uses three fingers to pluck the strings [(6)] are made out of silk on the movable bridge.

(4) (A) what	(B) who	(C) whose	(D) that
(5) (A) which	(B) that	(C) who	(D) what
(6) (A) who	(B) whom	(C) which	(D) each

Rome was not built in a day. [proverb]

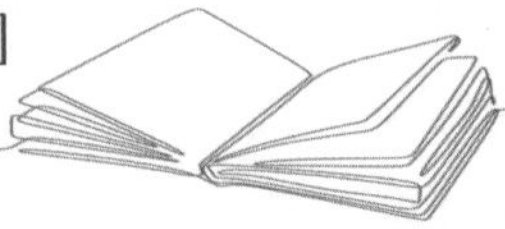

Part 3

Texts such as notices, letters and instant messages are followed by two or three questions. Choose the best answer to each question.

[1] Questions (1) and (2) refer to the following advertisement.

East of Paris

A fusion of French and Chinese cuisine.

Saturday 19th May

Pre-opening party 7 P.M. - 10 P.M.

Come and sample some highlights from the menu. Special price £10. Dinner service will begin from Friday 25th May. Reservations can be made online or by phone. Reservations made for the opening night will receive a 25% discount.

(1) What is the advertisement for?

(A) A French café
(B) A new restaurant
(C) A concert
(D) A Chinese buffet

(2) Who will get a discounted meal?

(A) People who go to the party on the 19th
(B) People who book online
(C) People who call in advance
(D) People who make a reservation for the 25th

[2] Questions (3) and (4) refer to the following notice.

Notice to Customers

Due to construction work on the entrance hall, the south entrance will be out of use for the next month. The entrance for the Bella Italian Restaurant is at the back of the building. Please use the stairs to the second floor. Regrettably, there is no wheel chair access as the lift will be closed during this time. For first floor shops, please use the east side entrance next to the bank.

We apologize for the inconvenience.

(3) Who is the notice for?

(A) Construction workers
(B) Building employees
(C) Restaurant staff
(D) Restaurant goers

(4) Which is NOT true about the Italian Restaurant?

(A) It is on the second floor.
(B) It will be closed for one month.
(C) The entrance is at the rear of the building.
(D) Wheelchair users cannot enter.

Unit 17 Stress

Grammar Target: Conditional Mood

Vocabulary Check 82

Listen to the following sentences and fill in the blanks.

(a) I (   ) I (   ) (   ) more time.

(b) He will (   ) (   ) to manager.

(c) Let's (   ) a (   ).

(d) I have (   ) how to (   ) (   ) stress.

(e) (   ) he (   ) (   ).

(f) Please (   ) my (   ).

Listening Section Practice

Part 1 83

[1] Choose the picture that the phrase or sentence best describes.

(A)

(B)

(C)

(D)

[2] Listen again to the sentence and fill in the blanks.

A girl (   ) (   ).

Part 2 84

[1] Listen to questions or statements. After each question or statement, you will hear and read four responses. Choose the best response.

(1) (A) We didn't. (B) That's a good idea.
(C) I often go there. (D) It's very warm.

(2) (A) I had fun. (B) No, I won't.
(C) I'd love to. (D) I'd go see my aunt.

(3) (A) She's with me. (B) I like the rainy season.
(C) You can use mine. (D) No, you don't.

(4) (A) Pass it over to me. (B) They're open on weekends.
(C) He went there. (D) I don't want any more trouble.

(5) (A) I bought a car. (B) I'd buy a house.
(C) Thank you very much. (D) No, I wouldn't.

[2] Listen again to each question or statement and fill in the blanks.

(1) (   ) (   ) we go for a hike (   ) it (   ) fine tomorrow?

(2) (   ) (   ) you visit (   ) you (   ) a long vacation?

(3) I (   ) I (   ) my umbrella (   ) me!

(4) I (   ) (   ) the company (   ) I (   ) you.

(5) (   ) (   ) you do (   ) you (   ) a lot of money?

Part 3 85

Listen to some short conversations. You will hear and read two questions about each conversation. Choose the best answer to each question.

[1] Questions (1) and (2) refer to the following conversation.

(1) How does the man look?
(A) Happy. (B) Excited. (C) Calm. (D) Upset.

(2) What are the man and woman going to do?
(A) Have coffee. (B) Play catch. (C) Take an exam. (D) Go for a picnic.

[2] Questions (3) and (4) refer to the following conversation.

(3) Why has the woman been busy?
(A) She changed her job. (B) She took a vacation.
(C) She skipped a meeting. (D) She got promoted.

(4) What does the woman want?
(A) A promotion. (B) A good sleep.
(C) A holiday. (D) A meeting.

Part 4 86

Listen to some short talks. You will hear and read two questions about each talk. Choose the best answer to each question.

[1] Questions (1) and (2) refer to the following talk.

(1) Who is the speaker?
- (A) A stress management trainer.
- (B) A trainee doctor.
- (C) A company trader.
- (D) A student.

(2) Why did the man quit his job?
- (A) Because it was stressful.
- (B) Because he was sick.
- (C) Because he wanted to help people.
- (D) Because he wanted to sleep more.

[2] Questions (3) and (4) refer to the following telephone message.

(3) What prevents the speaker from going to work?
- (A) She is tired.
- (B) She has a meeting.
- (C) She doesn't have any clients.
- (D) She has a headache.

(4) What will the woman do after this phone call?
- (A) Send a report.
- (B) E-mail clients.
- (C) Go back to work.
- (D) Go to the doctor.

Strategies for TOEIC BRIDGE #7

Listening Part 4 – Talks

In this section you will be asked two or three questions about a monologue. As in Part 3, try to read the questions and answer choices before the listening begins.

Reading Section Practice

Part 1

Each sentence has a space where a word or phrase is missing. Choose the best answer to complete the sentence.

(1) Lucy sounded as if she __________ a cold.
(A) were (B) take (C) did (D) had

(2) If you __________ to lose your job, how would you live?
(A) are (B) were (C) would be (D) had been

(3) I wish I __________ the advice from my boss.
(A) follow (B) will follow (C) would follow (D) had followed

(4) If I had finished the work earlier, I __________ to the ballgame.
(A) go (B) would go (C) went (D) could have gone

(5) __________ her, I could never have got this job.
(A) But for (B) Suppose (C) Given (D) In case of

(6) If the president __________ absent, the meeting will be postponed.
(A) is (B) was (C) were (D) would be

(7) It's time you __________ the office.
(A) are leaving (B) would leave (C) left (D) have left

(8) If it __________ not for his help, I would burst into tears.
(A) be (B) were (C) have (D) had

Part 2

Each of the short texts has three spaces where a word or phrase is missing. For each space, choose the best answer to complete the text.

[1] Questions (1) to (3) refer to the following article.

When you get angry…

Anger is a powerful feeling. It happens when you are stressed out, irritated, hurt, or disappointed. Anger can either help or hurt you, depending on how you deal with it. If you can [(1)] to it without hurting someone else, it can be a positive feeling. [(2)] you hold your anger inside you, it can lead to negative behavior such as attacking people. [(3)] learning how to express these feelings in the right way, you can control anger, solve problems, and hold on to important relationships. It is recommended that you keep a journal of when you feel angry.

(1) (A) help (B) get (C) hope (D) react
(2) (A) While (B) Although (C) If (D) Until
(3) (A) Of (B) If (C) When (D) By

[2] Questions (4) to (6) refer to the following article.

Can't Sleep?

If you can't sleep or you're feeling fatigued all day, there are some ways to cope. Taking a nap and drinking caffeinated beverages will help you keep alert during the day [(4)] interfering with your sleep at night.

Sleeping for a short time can make you more energetic. It increases your productivity during the day. Most people feel refreshed after taking a nap. It should last no more than 20 minutes. If your nap is [(5)] than that, it can be difficult to wake up from a deep sleep. It's also important not to nap late in the day because this can make it hard to fall asleep at night. Even a short nap in the early evening can interfere with bedtime.

[(6)] you drink coffee or tea, it is better to take them in the morning than in the afternoon. Consuming these drinks in the afternoon and evening can make it hard for you to fall asleep.

(4) (A) with (B) without (C) besides (D) for
(5) (A) less (B) shorter (C) longer (D) worse
(6) (A) If (B) However (C) But (D) While

Part 3

Texts such as notices, letters and instant messages are followed by two or three questions. Choose the best answer to each question.

[1] Questions (1) and (2) refer to the following article.

A new study has shown that most sick days taken by company employees are because of stress. Companies are losing money for a problem that can be solved. The study outlines steps that companies can take to help their employees stay healthy. These include simple measures such as improving the office environment by having more plants and offering yoga classes before work starts. There are more unusual suggestions such as employees bringing their pets to the office.

(1) Why are companies losing money?
- (A) Because employees don't work hard.
- (B) Because of problems with the system.
- (C) Because there is no sick pay.
- (D) Because employees are stressed.

(2) Which idea to help employees is NOT suggested?
- (A) More greenery in the office
- (B) Allow dogs at work
- (C) Morning yoga
- (D) Step exercises

[2] Questions (3) and (4) refer to the following online chat conversation.

Lucy: Hi! How have you been recently? Last time we met, you said you hadn't been feeling very well. Are you feeling better now?

Corrine: Yes, I'm a bit better. Thanks. I was really busy at work. I think it was stress. I started walking to work which has helped.

Lucy: That's good. If I were you, I would start taking a yoga class. It really helped my stress last year when I was taking my exams.

Corrine: That's a great idea, thanks. Are you still taking the class?

Lucy: Yes, I might go tonight. If I go, I'll call you. Right, I have to work now!

(3) Why was Lucy stressed?
- (A) She was busy.
- (B) She didn't go to yoga.
- (C) She had a test.
- (D) She had to work.

(4) Why will Lucy call Corrine?
- (A) To invite her to a class
- (B) To check she is OK
- (C) To help with an exam
- (D) To help with work

Unit 18 Ghosts

Grammar Target: Past and Present Perfect Tense

Vocabulary Check

87

Listen to the following sentences and fill in the blanks.

(a) I've (   ) (   ) (   ) before.

(b) (   ) you (   ) (   ) a tiger?

(c) You (   ) to (   ) (   ) a tough time.

(d) A lot of vegetables (   ) (   ) here.

(e) You can (   ) and (   ) cows.

(f) (   ) you (   ) your (   ).

Listening Section Practice

Part 1 88

[1] Choose the picture that the phrase or sentence best describes.

(A)

(B)

(C)

(D)

[2] Listen again to the sentence and fill in the blanks.

A bird (   ) (   ) in the (   ).

Part 2 89

[1] Listen to questions or statements. After each question or statement, you will hear and read four responses. Choose the best response.

(1) (A) Once in a while. (B) Yes, I will.
(C) Did you? (D) No, you weren't.

(2) (A) I like green. (B) Did you ever do it?
(C) I've been there several times. (D) I'll turn the heat on.

(3) (A) How was it? (B) Visitors only.
(C) Is he from Spain? (D) You're welcome.

(4) (A) She loves swimming. (B) In the swimming pool.
(C) On the beach. (D) Me, either.

(5) (A) I'll call you. (B) He's on the phone right now.
(C) Look up in the phone book. (D) Yes. I don't need one.

[2] Listen again to each question or statement and fill in the blanks.

(1) I (   ) a dolphin (   ) the (   ) time.
(2) (   ) you (   ) (   ) to Greece?
(3) I finally (   ) a (   ) to (   ) Spain.
(4) I (   ) (   ) (   ) at the beach.
(5) Is it (   ) that you've (   ) (   ) a mobile phone?

Part 3 90

Listen to some short conversations. You will hear and read two questions about each conversation. Choose the best answer to each question.

[1] Questions (1) and (2) refer to the following conversation.

(1) What is the woman afraid of?
(A) Getting lost. (B) Meeting her.
(C) Having arrived too early. (D) Living alone.

(2) What is her impression of the neighborhood?
(A) Noisy. (B) Huge. (C) Quiet. (D) Dangerous.

[2] Questions (3) and (4) refer to the following conversation.

(3) What does the woman gaze into?
(A) A tough time. (B) A cookie.
(C) The man's eyes. (D) A tea cup.

(4) What does the woman advise the man to do?
(A) Go through hardship. (B) Find a way.
(C) Follow his own heart. (D) Drink tea.

The most important thing in communication is hearing what isn't said.
[Peter Drucker]

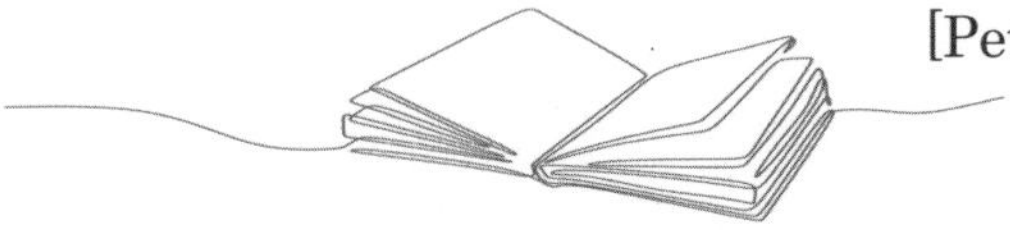

Part 4 91

Listen to some short talks. You will hear and read two questions about each talk. Choose the best answer to each question.

[1] Questions (1) and (2) refer to the following talk.

(1) Where do the vegetables for the café come from?
(A) From the local market.
(B) From the supermarket.
(C) From the front garden.
(D) From the kitchen garden.

(2) What can the visitors try to do?
(A) Harvest the wheat.
(B) Milk the cows.
(C) Pick herbs in the garden.
(D) Cook vegetables in the café.

[2] Questions (3) and (4) refer to the following telephone message.

(3) Who is speaking?
(A) A cinema manager.
(B) A new member of staff.
(C) A movie goer.
(D) A movie critic.

(4) What will the listener do on Friday?
(A) Watch a movie.
(B) Take an interview.
(C) Start a new job.
(D) Call the manager.

Reading Section Practice

Part 1

Each sentence has a space where a word or phrase is missing. Choose the best answer to complete the sentence.

(1) _________ you ever seen a pyramid?
(A) Are (B) Do (C) Did (D) Have

(2) _________ you have any trouble getting here?
(A) Are (B) Did (C) Have (D) If

(3) I have _________ to the North Pole many times.
(A) had (B) been (C) came (D) done

(4) I have _________ called an ambulance in my life.
(A) ever (B) still (C) yet (D) never

(5) Have they ever _________ raw fish?
(A) eat (B) eats (C) ate (D) eaten

(6) _________ John ever tried to play this game?
(A) Is (B) Was (C) Has (D) Does

(7) _________ Simon come to the office yesterday?
(A) Is (B) Does (C) Did (D) has

(8) I _________ my car key on the way home last night.
(A) lose (B) lost (C) will lose (D) have lost

Part 2

Each of the short texts has three spaces where a word or phrase is missing. For each space, choose the best answer to complete the text.

[1] Questions (1) to (3) refer to the following advertisement.

Send Us Your Unique Photos

We are offering you the chance to share your photos [(1)] us and other readers. [(2)] you ever seen a UFO or any unidentified mysterious animals? If you're lucky enough to photograph them, share them with us! Here's what to do!

1. Take the picture with your cellphone or digital camera.
2. Send it to ufopix@dailynews.com
3. Include your name and [(3)] a brief description of the photo.

(1) (A) for	(B) to	(C) among	(D) with
(2) (A) Are	(B) Were	(C) Have	(D) Did
(3) (A) fly	(B) see	(C) add	(D) take

[2] Questions (4) to (6) refer to the following article.

Tip of the week: How to survive in the wild

Have you ever [(4)] lost in the forest? Can you imagine what it would be like to be completely on your own? If you want to survive in wilderness, the first thing you need to know is that you always need to be well prepared. You [(5)] not go in the woods without water, a knife, and fire starter. Even if you don't plan to go into the wild, you still need to be prepared with survival gear. It's a good idea to keep an emergency kit in your car in case accidents happen.

There are only three things that you need in order to survive in the wild [(6)] you're sick or seriously injured. These are water, food, and warmth. If you are ever lost in the forest with nothing, just follow these steps....

(4) (A) had	(B) got	(C) caught	(D) done
(5) (A) are	(B) have	(C) had	(D) must
(6) (A) when	(B) before	(C) nonetheless	(D) unless

Part 3

Texts such as notices, letters and instant messages are followed by two or three questions. Choose the best answer to each question.

[1] Questions (1) and (2) refer to the following advertisement.

Halloween Horror Movie Marathon!

31st October, 8 P.M. to 1 A.M.

Come enjoy the scariest night of the year.

We will be showing three classic horror films.
Book tickets in advance online $20. On the door $26 (3D glasses with no charge).
There will be a special gift for those who come in costume.

(1) What will people do on 31st of October?
(A) Run a marathon
(B) Watch horror movies
(C) See a scary ghost
(D) Go to a Halloween party

(2) What is included in the ticket price?
(A) A special gift
(B) 3D glasses
(C) A free movie
(D) A costume

[2] Questions (3) and (4) refer to the following online chat conversation.

Toby: So, I'm off to Vietnam next week. What are you doing this summer?

Rob: That sounds exciting. I'm going to India. Have you ever been there?

Toby: Yes, I have. I loved it. You'll have a great time. When are you leaving?

Rob: The day after tomorrow. I'll be there for two weeks. Do you have any advice?

Toby: Don't drink the tap water. Don't eat any salads, and be sure to wash your hands.

(3) When is Rob going to India?
(A) Tomorrow
(B) In two days
(C) Next week
(D) In two weeks

(4) What should Rob do?
(A) Drink tap water
(B) Eat lots of salad
(C) Wash his clothes
(D) Keep his hands clean

Unit 19 Housing

Grammar Target: Participial Adjectives

Vocabulary Check 92

Listen to the following sentences and fill in the blanks.

(a) The ( ) is very ( ).

(b) We ( ) ( ) help.

(c) The police ( ) not ( ) the ( ).

(d) Please ( ) ( ) of ( ) people.

(e) Please ( ) all the doors ( ).

(f) There is a ( ) ( ) ( ).

Listening Section Practice

Part 1 93

[1] Choose the picture that the phrase or sentence best describes.

(A)

(B)

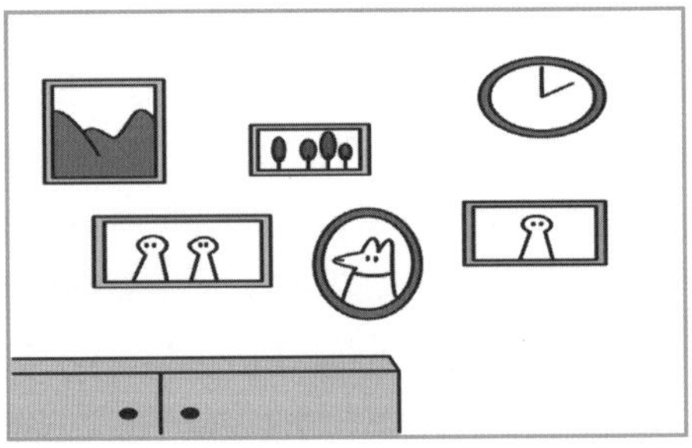

(C)

(D)

[2] Listen again to the sentence and fill in the blanks.

Many ( ) ( ) on the ( ).

Part 2 94

[1] Listen to questions or statements. After each question or statement, you will hear and read four responses. Choose the best response.

(1) (A) It matches your suit. (B) I will import them.
(C) Thank you. (D) In my office.

(2) (A) I'm fine. (B) Yes, I did.
(C) I work very hard. (D) It is relaxing.

(3) (A) Yes, I spend most of my time in there.
(B) Do you walk to school?
(C) Yes, I bought them at a garage sale.
(D) Here's my driving license.

(4) (A) I looked for it. (B) She's with us.
(C) Yes, I will. (D) I moved the furniture myself.

(5) (A) Yes, I do. (B) So am I.
(C) You're an interesting teacher. (D) She's out in the garden.

[2] Listen again to each question or statement and fill in the blanks.

(1) The (　　　) you have (　　　) your room is (　　　).
(2) (　　　) (　　　) you (　　　) your new office?
(3) It's (　　　) to (　　　) a (　　　), isn't it?
(4) You (　　　) (　　　).
(5) I'm (　　　) (　　　) gardening.

Part 3 95

Listen to some short conversations. You will hear and read two questions about each conversation. Choose the best answer to each question.

[1] Questions (1) and (2) refer to the following conversation.

(1) What does the man say about the woman's room?
(A) Thrilling. (B) Exciting. (C) Comfortable. (D) Large.

(2) What does the man advise the woman to do?
(A) Go out for a walk. (B) Clean the room.
(C) Sleep well. (D) Study in the library.

[2] Questions (3) and (4) refer to the following conversation.

(3) How does the man look?
(A) Tired. (B) Excited. (C) Busy. (D) Sad.

(4) What is suggested about moving companies?
(A) They are content.
(B) They are satisfied.
(C) They are refreshed.
(D) They are busy.

Part 4 96

Listen to some short talks. You will hear and read two questions about each talk. Choose the best answer to each question.

[1] Questions (1) and (2) refer to the following talk.

(1) Who is the speaker talking to?
(A) A group of neighbors.
(B) TV announcers.
(C) Jewelry shop owners.
(D) The police.

(2) What is the meeting about?
(A) Damaged houses.
(B) How to save money.
(C) Broken gates.
(D) Crime in the area.

[2] Questions (3) and (4) refer to the following telephone message.

(3) What does the woman want to do?
(A) Order a newspaper.
(B) Place an advertisement.
(C) Get a full-time job.
(D) View a room.

(4) What does the women ask the listener to do?
(A) Lower the price.
(B) Visit on weekends.
(C) Return a phone call.
(D) Look after a cat.

Reading Section Practice

Part 1

Each sentence has a space where a word or phrase is missing. Choose the best answer to complete the sentence.

(1) She is very ________ with her new house.
(A) satisfy (B) satisfying (C) satisfied (D) satisfaction

(2) It's ________ to see movies in the theater.
(A) excite (B) exciting (C) excited (D) excitement

(3) You look ________ staying in your room all day.
(A) bore (B) boring (C) bored (D) boredom

(4) I find it ________ to look for a piece of nice furniture.
(A) interest (B) interests (C) interested (D) interesting

(5) Are you ________ in designing rooms?
(A) happy (B) building (C) thrilling (D) interested

(6) I was ________ to notice that her house had no curtains.
(A) surprise (B) surprising (C) surprised (D) surprisingly

(7) It's not ________ that Ronny turned into a minimalist.
(A) surprise (B) surprises (C) surprising (D) surprised

(8) Cindy was ________ when she found her new sofa too large to fit in her room.
(A) disappoint (B) disappointment (C) disappointing (D) disappointed

Part 2

Each of the short texts has three spaces where a word or phrase is missing. For each space, choose the best answer to complete the text.

[1] Questions (1) to (3) refer to the following article.

Make Your Bedroom Comfortable

Most studies suggest that sleep is the most important activity to keep you healthy. Therefore, your bedroom is the most important (1) in your house. You need to make it a (2) environment. Also, you need your bedroom to be arranged in a functional way so that you can move around the space as you go through your daily routine. For example, it is recommended that you (3) at least 60 cm between the sides of the bed and the wall.

(1) (A) furniture (B) interior (C) design (D) space
(2) (A) satisfied (B) tiring (C) relaxing (D) entertained
(3) (A) fall (B) measure (C) increase (D) keep

[2] Questions (4) to (6) refer to the following note.

Tips for Purchasing Furniture at Garage Sales

Shopping at garage sales in your neighborhood can be an (4) pastime. However, it is different from shopping at a mall or a local shop. Of course you usually get a second hand furniture there. So you should have some knowledge to inspect the conditions of furniture before you (5) to buy. People often end up buying furniture without careful inspection, only to be (6) once they bring a piece home. For example, you need to check the legs on chairs are sturdy.

(4) (A) interesting (B) amazed (C) irritated (D) overcrowded
(5) (A) forget (B) remember (C) are (D) decide
(6) (A) disappointed (B) filled (C) covered (D) satisfied

Part 3

Texts such as notices, letters and instant messages are followed by two or three questions. Choose the best answer to each question.

[1] Questions (1) and (2) refer to the following article.

Here's a simple way to improve your indoor environment. Research has shown that plants are the best way to keep the air in your house clean. Some of the most effective air purifiers are ivy, aloe and spider plants. Studies also have shown that plants in a room can reduce stress, improve mood, concentration, and memory. Introducing a little green into your life may make a big difference!

---

(1) What is the article mainly about?
- (A) How to improve your room
- (B) How to enrich your life
- (C) How to start a garden
- (D) How to save the environment

(2) What is stated about plants?
- (A) Plants can increase stress.
- (B) Plants purify the air.
- (C) They can make aloe juice.
- (D) Spiders like plants.

[2] Questions (3) and (4) refer to the following text message.

Jane: Hi. I finished work early today. I haven't made dinner yet, but I've been having a big declutter. Could you pick up some rubbish bags on your way home?

Steve: ______________________________

(3) What has Jane been doing?
- (A) Cleaning her bags
- (B) Cooking a big dinner
- (C) Throwing away unnecessary items
- (D) Finishing her work

(4) Select the best response to Jane's message.
- (A) I don't have any rubbish.
- (B) Did you finish working?
- (C) Sure, no problems. Good work.
- (D) Sure, I left my bag at home.

Unit 20 Gender Equality

Grammar Target: Indirect Questions

Vocabulary Check 97

Listen to the following sentences and fill in the blanks.

(a) I (   ) my (   ) every night.

(b) Please (   ) me (   ) you (   ) the company.

(c) We (   ) (   ).

(d) There (   ) a lot of (   ) (   ) careers.

(e) She (   ) some time (   ).

(f) I have been (   ) (   ) in (   ).

Listening Section Practice

Part 1 98

[1] Choose the picture that the phrase or sentence best describes.

(A)

(B)

(C)

(D)

[2] Listen again to the sentence and fill in the blanks.

A man (   ) (   ) in the kitchen.

Part 2 99

[1] Listen to questions or statements. After each question or statement, you will hear and read four responses. Choose the best response.

(1) (A) He works very hard. (B) It's my birthday today.
(C) Next month. (D) Yes, he does.

(2) (A) My friend may be interested in it. (B) We'll have a workshop next week.
(C) He's always with us. (D) I've worked for a long time.

(3) (A) Sorry, I'm late. (B) It started at two.
(C) You can say that again. (D) He was taking care of his son.

(4) (A) Are you leaving? (B) I heard she left home at seven.
(C) She took some photographs. (D) I heard she took only a month's leave.

(5) (A) Our consultant will help you. (B) I asked for water.
(C) I'm happy with it. (D) It's well-balanced.

[2] Listen again to each question or statement and fill in the blanks.

(1) Do you ( ) ( ) Fred ( ) back to work?

(2) My boss ( ) me if ( ) ( ) anyone who wanted to work with us.

(3) Can you ( ) me ( ) Brian ( ) late for the meeting?

(4) Does anyone ( ) ( ) ( ) Jane ( ) for maternity leave?

(5) Please ( ) me ( ) I ( ) ( ) to ask for advice on work-life balance.

Part 3 100

Listen to some short conversations. You will hear and read two questions about each conversation. Choose the best answer to each question.

[1] Questions (1) and (2) refer to the following conversation.

(1) How long was the man's paternity leave?
(A) For a week. (B) For a month. (C) For half a year. (D) For a year.

(2) What does the man think about his paternity leave?
(A) It was tough. (B) It was wonderful. (C) It was too short. (D) It was boring.

[2] Questions (3) and (4) refer to the following conversation.

(3) Why did the woman quit her job?
(A) She didn't get along with her boss. (B) She was not happy with the pay.
(C) She was headhunted. (D) She didn't like working.

(4) What is the woman doing now?
(A) She is launching a company. (B) She is leaving the company.
(C) She is meeting her boss. (D) She is looking for a job.

Genius is 1 percent inspiration, 99 percent perspiration.
[Thomas Alva Edison]

Part 4 101

Listen to some short talks. You will hear and read two questions about each talk. Choose the best answer to each question.

[1] Questions (1) and (2) refer to the following talk.

(1) What has changed for women?
(A) They don't want to have a career.
(B) They have children in their 20's.
(C) They have children when they are older.
(D) They don't want to have children.

(2) What is the problem with paternity leave?
(A) It is part of promotion.
(B) Men take it too often.
(C) It is not manly.
(D) Men don't take it.

[2] Questions (3) and (4) refer to the following telephone message.

(3) What is the appointment for?
(A) Work. (B) Doctor. (C) School. (D) Dentist.

(4) What does the man want to do?
(A) Cancel his appointment.
(B) Drive to work.
(C) Reschedule his appointment.
(D) Avoid traffic.

Reading Section Practice

Part 1

Each sentence has a space where a word or phrase is missing. Choose the best answer to complete the sentence.

(1) (1) Do you know why Jerry ________ home early?
(A) have (B) go (C) come (D) left

(2) I ________ my boss if I could take a few days off.
(A) was (B) asked (C) know (D) like

(3) Who can tell if we ________ full equality of rights between men and women?
(A) are achieved (B) be achieving (C) achieves (D) could achieve

(4) Did Clare tell you when she ________ going to come back to work?
(A) is (B) was (C) do (D) did

(5) Alex asked me ________ my wife was working.
(A) whether (B) which (C) who (D) to

(6) Nobody told me why Mr. Martin ________ my work.
(A) will be (B) have taken (C) do (D) had praised

(7) Could you tell us ________ there's a childcare facility in the building?
(A) if (B) how (C) what (D) who

(8) I don't know how long Linda ________ as a secretary.
(A) work (B) working (C) is worked (D) has worked

Part 2

Each of the short texts has three spaces where a word or phrase is missing. For each space, choose the best answer to complete the text.

[1] Questions (1) to (3) refer to the following note.

History of Suffragettes in America

Do you know [(1)] women in American finally gained the right to vote? Also, do you know what women's suffrage [(2)] ?

Up until the Nineteenth Amendment was passed in 1920, women were [(3)] to vote. After many years of suffragettes fighting for their rights, the right to vote was given to women in America.

(1) (A) who	(B) which	(C) when	(D) how long
(2) (A) do	(B) too	(C) by	(D) means
(3) (A) right	(B) pleased	(C) lucky	(D) unable

[2] Questions (4) to (6) refer to the following article.

Want to be a babysitter?

Many people ask [(4)] skills they need to become a babysitter. First, you need to decide if babysitting is really the right choice for you, based on your personal situation and interests. So, ask [(5)] if you really like children and if you have time to babysit. If you find you really want to babysit, then you should start [(6)] taking a babysitting course and First Aid training. Finally, you'll be ready to find your first babysitting job.

(4) (A) who	(B) what	(C) when	(D) how
(5) (A) him	(B) mine	(C) ours	(D) yourself
(6) (A) to	(B) without	(C) between	(D) by

Part 3

Texts such as notices, letters and instant messages are followed by two or three questions. Choose the best answer to each question.

[1] Questions (1) and (2) refer to the following advertisement.

Clothes Swap

Saturday 16th May

St. John's Church Hall

Buying toys and children's clothes can be expensive, especially when they grow so quickly. We are holding our bi-yearly spring session at ST John's Church Hall. It's a great place to meet other parents if you are new to the area. Tea and cakes will be on offer to make the morning sociable. The next event will be in autumn.

Bring any children's clothes, toys, cots, anything you don't use any more. All ages welcome. Take home what you need for the next year.

(1) How often is this event held?
  (A) Every Saturday morning
  (B) Once a month
  (C) Once a year
  (D) Twice a year

(2) What is NOT available in this event?
  (A) Vehicles
  (B) Tea
  (C) Cakes
  (D) Clothes

[2] Questions (3) and (4) refer to the following text message.

Akiko: How are you? I haven't seen you for ages. How are you feeling? How is maternity leave going? When will you be coming back to work?

Liz: ____

(3) What is suggested about Liz?
  (A) She has never worked.
  (B) She is working now.
  (C) She had a baby.
  (D) She is sick.

(4) Select the best response to Akiko's message.
  (A) "Fine, thanks. I haven't got a new job yet."
  (B) "Good, thanks. I've been busy working."
  (C) "Fine, thanks. I'm looking for a job."
  (D) "Good, thanks. I am due back next month."

Strategies for TOEIC BRIDGE #8

Time Management Tip for TOEIC Bridge

TOEIC BRIDGE is a 60-minute examination. You need to use your time wisely as well as keep your concentration in order to complete the test in time.

For the Listening sections, especially for Part 3 and Part 4, keep yourself busy! Make sure you pre-read, but don't get left behind or you may miss important information related to the next question. For the Reading section, try to answer all questions in Part 1 as quickly as possible so you can spend more time on Part 2 and Part 3.

TOEIC BRIDGE SAMPLE TEST

Listening Section: This is the Listening test. There are four parts to this test.

Part 1 102

You will see a set of four pictures in your book, and you will hear one short phrase or sentence. Look at the set of pictures. Choose the picture that the phrase or sentence best describes. Then mark the letter (A), (B), (C), or (D) on your answer sheet.

1. (A)

(B)

(C)

(D)

2. (A)

(B)

(C)

(D)

3. (A)

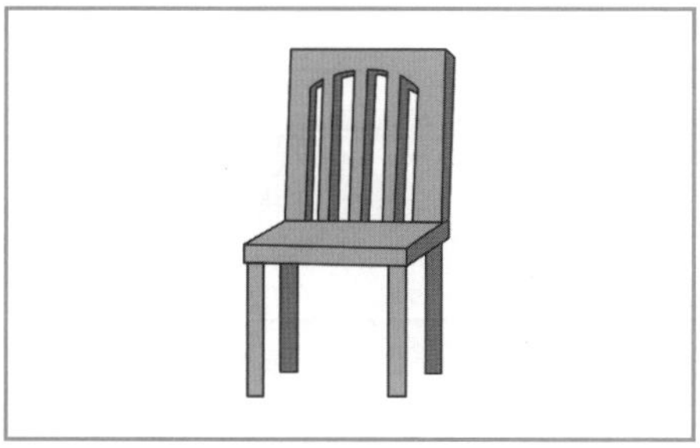

(B)

(C)

(D)

4. (A)

(B)

(C)

(D)

5. (A)

(B)

(C)

(D)

6. (A)

(B)

(C)

(D)

Part 2 103

You will hear some questions or statements. After each question or statement, you will hear and read four responses. Choose the best response to each question or statement. Then mark the letter (A), (B), (C), or (D) on your answer sheet.

7. (A) I'm watching TV.
(B) Very well, and you?
(C) It's raining.
(D) He's out now.

8. (A) It's for you.
(B) Very good.
(C) I ate some.
(D) My mother did.

9. (A) He's from America.
(B) I'm fine, thank you.
(C) Nice to meet you.
(D) Here you are.

10. (A) Yes, you were.
(B) Is this yours?
(C) It's my helmet.
(D) Did you?

11. (A) Yes, I'm tired today.
(B) I usually sleep for seven hours.
(C) I went to bed at eleven.
(D) I went out last night.

12. (A) She looked for him.
(B) Look at me.
(C) I didn't sleep well.
(D) I got a flat tire.

13. (A) Since this morning.
(B) Yes, I have.
(C) I've been tired.
(D) It takes two hours.

14. (A) I managed it.
(B) Will you introduce me to him?
(C) I hope he will.
(D) It's a new one.

15. (A) I'm in a hurry.
(B) No use.
(C) I went there, too.
(D) It's my pleasure.

16. (A) I walked.
(B) It's by the door.
(C) He's coming.
(D) It was cloudy.

17. (A) Sorry, I'm busy.
(B) Yes, she is.
(C) No, you're not.
(D) I went there with her.

18. (A) Yes, several times.
(B) Yes, it's allowed.
(C) No, there isn't.
(D) It's been hot these days.

19. (A) I saw it on TV.
(B) See you tomorrow.
(C) Because I want it.
(D) Yes, let's.

20. (A) Last month.
(B) How about on Saturday?
(C) Yes, we did.
(D) No, they aren't.

21. (A) Because it's there.
(B) Nice to see you again.
(C) I got caught in a traffic jam.
(D) I don't eat meat.

22. (A) In the library.
(B) Yes, he's interesting.
(C) Sooner or later.
(D) It's in the history book.

23. (A) I like reading books.
(B) You'll hear it.
(C) Yes, there's one around the corner.
(D) I don't have any books.

24. (A) Can I have a cup of tea?
(B) On the table.
(C) For an hour.
(D) No, she isn't.

25. (A) I've had enough.
(B) Last night.
(C) Yes, I'll buy some tomorrow.
(D) Sure, here you are.

26. (A) I usually walk.
(B) By car.
(C) I often watch TV.
(D) No. I want to see it.

Part 3 104

You will hear some short conversations. You will hear and read two questions about each conversation. Each question has four answer choices. Choose the best answer to each question and mark the letter (A), (B), (C), or (D) on your answer sheet.

Questions 27 and 28 refer to the following conversation.

27. Where are the speakers?
(A) At a hotel. (B) At a library. (C) At a supermarket. (D) At a restaurant.

28. Where does the woman want to go?
(A) To a coffee shop. (B) To a gym. (C) To a theater. (D) To the post office.

Questions 29 and 30 refer to the following conversation.

29. What does the woman want to buy?
(A) Water. (B) Juice. (C) Soda. (D) Wine.

30. How much will the woman pay?
(A) $6.00. (B) $12.00. (C) $12.50. (D) $20.00.

Questions 31 and 32 refer to the following conversation.

31. Where are the speakers?
(A) At a hotel. (B) At a museum. (C) At the airport. (D) At a bank.

32. How many days will the woman be in the country?
(A) One day. (B) Three days. (C) Five days. (D) Seven days.

Questions 33 and 34 refer to the following conversation and list.

Undergraduate	10 books	for 3 weeks
Graduate	25 books	for 1 month
Teachers	50 books	for 2 months
People from outside the Univ.	5 books	for 1 week

33. Who is the man?
(A) A teacher. (B) A scientist. (C) A librarian. (D) A shop clerk.

34. How many books can the woman borrow at a time?
(A) Up to 5 books. (B) Up to 10 books. (C) Up to 25 books. (D) Up to 50 books.

Questions 35 and 36 refer to the following conversation and list.

35. How many muffins will the woman buy?
(A) One. (B) Two. (C) Three. (D) Four.

36. How much is the total?
(A) $3.00. (B) $5.00. (C) $7.50. (D) $10.50.

Handmade Muffin	$3.00 for 1
	$5.00 for 2
	$7.50 for 3
Iced Coffee	$2.00
Iced Tea	$1.50

Part 4 105

You will hear some short talks. You will hear and read two questions about each talk. Each question has four answer choices. Choose the best answer to each question and mark the letter (A), (B), (C), or (D) on your answer sheet.

Questions 37 and 38 refer to the following talk.

37. Who is the speaker?
(A) A teacher.
(B) A camera salesman.
(C) A student.
(D) A gardener.

38. What will they do today?
(A) Plant flowers.
(B) Design a garden.
(C) Lean to use a camera.
(D) Take a walk.

Questions 39 and 40 refer to the following announcement.

39. What is the final destination of the bus?
(A) London.
(B) Wincheston.
(C) Rochdale.
(D) Ludwell Airport.

40. When will the bus leave?
(A) In 10 minutes.
(B) In 15 minutes.
(C) At 10:45.
(D) At 11:30.

Questions 41 and 42 refer to the following telephone message.

41. Who is the speaker?
(A) A shop assistant.
(B) A customer service worker.
(C) A delivery man.
(D) A repair man.

42. What does the listener want?
(A) A reply to mail.
(B) A new copy machine.
(C) A new engineer.
(D) A copy machine repaired.

Questions 43 and 44 refer to the following telephone message.

43. What does the speaker want?
(A) To rent a house.
(B) To buy a bigger washing machine.
(C) To look at a new house.
(D) To sell a washing machine.

44. What does the woman ask the listener to do?
(A) Pick up the washing machine today.
(B) Look at the advertisement.
(C) Deliver a washing machine.
(D) Leave the house tomorrow.

Questions 45 and 46 refer to the following talk.

45. Who is the speaker?
(A) A cook. (B) A waiter. (C) A bartender. (D) A manager.

46. What will the listeners do next?
(A) Prepare dinner. (B) Serve food. (C) Change clothes. (D) Offer drinks.

Questions 47 and 48 refer to the following telephone message and price list.

Lockheath Forest Campsite - Price List

Price per night	Tent Pitch	Caravan Pitch
Off Peak Nov - Mar	£ 6	£10
Apr-Jun Sep-Oct	£10	£14
High Season Jul-Aug	£14	£18

Booking made by telephone only from 10 A.M. to 5 P.M. weekdays.

47. What will the caller do later?
(A) Call the campsite.
(B) Buy a tent.
(C) Make a caravan reservation.
(D) Check the prices online.

48. How much will the caller need to pay to the camp?
(A) £18. (B) £28. (C) £30. (D) £42.

Questions 49 and 50 refer to the following radio advertisement and sign.

Help Wanted in Busy Florists

Early morning shift 6 A.M. - 8 A.M.
Afternoon shift 1 P.M. - 3 P.M.

49. What is the advertisement for?
(A) A job in a flower shop.
(B) Working at home.
(C) Kids flower arrangement lessons.
(D) A course to study flowers.

50. What time could a stay at home parent start work?
(A) 6 A.M. (B) 8 A.M. (C) 1 P.M. (D) 3 P.M.

Reading Section: This is the Reading test. There are three parts to this test. You will have 35 minutes to complete the Reading test.

Part 1

You will read some sentences. Each one has a space where a word or phrase is missing. Choose the best answer to complete the sentence. Then mark the letter (A), (B), (C), or (D) on your answer sheet.

51. There _________ a lot of children in the park yesterday.
(A) is (B) are (C) was (D) were

52. He is _________ London, England.
(A) below (B) from (C) beneath (D) above

53. Cindy has a brother _________ studies abroad.
(A) who (B) which (C) where (D) whose

54. He can _________ very well.
(A) cook (B) cooks (C) cooked (D) cooking

55 Would you teach my son _________ to ride a bicycle?
(A) who (B) what (C) how (D) why

56. Don is a _________ car sales man in his hometown.
(A) success (B) successful (C) successfully (D) succeed

57. Buses leaving for Boston _________ delayed due to the snow.
(A) is (B) are (C) should (D) must

58. The soccer match was very _________.
(A) excite (B) excited (C) exciting (D) excitement

59. Where did you visit _________ your holidays?
(A) during (B) when (C) though (D) while

60. Using a mobile phone while driving _________ strictly prohibited.
(A) be (B) is (C) are (D) been

61. It _________ cold since last week.
(A) is (B) was (C) will be (D) has been

62. Thank you very much _________ coming to my place.
(A) when (B) by (C) to (D) for

63. I went to the grocery store _________ I needed to buy some water.
(A) although (B) because (C) unless (D) despite

64. It is _________ for Tom to speak in front of many people.
(A) kind (B) easy (C) amazed (D) fluently

65. Everyone in the class enjoyed _________ the movie.
(A) watch (B) to watch (C) watched (D) watching

Part 2

You will read some short texts. Each one has three spaces where a word, phrase, or sentence is missing. For each space, choose the best answer to complete the text. Then mark the letter (A), (B), (C), or (D) on your answer sheet.

Questions 66 to 68 refer to the following letter.

Emily,

It was so much fun (66) dinner with you. I (67) I can see you again soon. When you (68) to this area again, please stop by.

Thanks.

Ben

66. (A) to have (B) have (C) had (D) have had
67. (A) need (B) let (C) make (D) hope
68. (A) go (B) come (C) visit (D) take

Questions 69 to 71 refer to the following notice.

Refrigerator Cleaning Day

The refrigerator (69) be cleaned out every Friday.

Please (70) to remove all personal items before you go home.

Everything remaining in the refrigerator will be thrown (71).

Thank you for your cooperation.

Manager

69. (A) may (B) will (C) won't (D) had to
70. (A) forget (B) remember (C) refrain (D) prevent
71. (A) in (B) forward (C) from (D) away

Questions 72 to 74 refer to the following notice.

Guitar-Loving-Club

Your Account will be deactivated in 30 days.

It looks [(72)] you haven't signed in to our website "Guitar-Loving-Club" for a while; (ID#7891234; Your account; jimmypageisgod) Guitar-Loving-Club accounts are automatically deactivated [(73)] 90 days of inactivity.

To keep your account open, please sign in [(74)] October 15, 2021.

If you need help, please contact us.

72. (A) at (B) for (C) into (D) like
73. (A) before (B) after (C) for (D) since
74. (A) by (B) from (C) in (D) for

Questions 75 to 77 refer to the following e-mail.

To: buchananengdept@leiscteruni.ac.uk
Subject: ENG102

Dear Dr. Buchanan,

This is Emily Turner from your English 102 class. I am very sorry for [(75)] class last Tuesday. I had a small car accident [(76)] my way to school that day. I am hoping you will give me the material I missed. I would [(77)] any help you might be able to give me.

Sincerely,
Emily Turner

75. (A) miss (B) missed (C) to miss (D) missing
76. (A) in (B) on (C) from (D) over
77. (A) duplicate (B) communicate (C) activate (D) appreciate

Questions 78 to 80 refer to the following notice.

Laundry Room Rules

For Residents use only

Be patient: Please [(78)] others 20-30 minutes after their cycle has finished to remove their clothes [(79)] the washer or dryer.

Be clean: Please [(80)] the laundry room neat. Be sure to clean up spilled detergent.

Be respectful: Please treat everyone's clothes like your own.

78.	(A) give	(B) take	(C) keep	(D) look
79.	(A) without	(B) away	(C) of	(D) from
80.	(A) wash	(B) keep	(C) stay	(D) dry

Part 3

You will read some texts such as notices, letters and instant message. Each text is followed by two or three questions. Choose the best answer to each question and mark the letter (A), (B), (C), or (D) on your answer sheet.

Questions 81 and 82 refer to the following text message.

Anna: Hi. Do you want to go shopping tomorrow morning? I need to get a birthday present for my mom. Can you help me choose? I can come pick you up at 10 A.M.

Louise: ____

81. What will Anna do first in the morning tomorrow?

(A) Go shopping
(B) Call her mom
(C) Go to her friend's house
(D) Send a birthday present

82. Select the best response to Anna's message.

(A) "Yes. I went shopping today, too!"
(B) "Sure. I can help your mom."
(C) "No. I haven't chosen a present yet."
(D) "Sure. I have a great idea!"

Questions 83 and 84 refer to the following notice.

Because of the plans to widen the old shopping street, many of the shops in Rockdale Town will be closing. Some will move to the new shopping center that will open next month. However, the ladies clothing store, Paradon, will close next week. Customers can pick up any ordered items until 1 P.M. on Friday. After that, orders will be transferred to the branch in Middleton Town.

83. Why is the shop closing?

(A) Because there is construction to the road.
(B) Because they didn't have any customers.
(C) Because it is moving to another location.
(D) Because they will open a new branch.

84. Where can customers receive their orders after Friday?

(A) The new shopping center
(B) The Rockdale branch
(C) The construction company
(D) The Middleton branch

Questions 85 and 86 refer to the following text message.

Phil: Hello! How did the job interview go? I finish early tonight. Do you want to meet up for a drink in that new bar in town tonight?

Colin: ______________________________

85. What is most likely true about Colin?
(A) He usually works late.
(B) He has a job in a bar.
(C) He is looking for a new job.
(D) He is leaving town.

86. Select the best response to Phil's message.
(A) "It was OK. And yes. See you later then!"
(B) "No. I can't go on Friday."
(C) "Yes. Please help me with the interview."
(D) "That sounds great. See you tomorrow!"

Questions 87 and 88 refer to the following advertisement.

Senior Smart Phone Classes

Do you have a new smart phone? Not sure how to use it? Come learn new skills to help keep you connected with younger people. Classes are for the over 65s only. It's easy to learn, no textbook necessary.

Venue: St. James Church Hall.
Time: Wednesday 7th July 10:30 A.M.
Price: £3

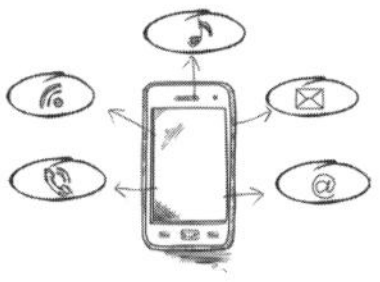

Bring snacks and we will provide the tea.

87. Who is the class for?
(A) People who don't have a smart phone
(B) People who can use smart phones
(C) Young people to learn job skills
(D) Older people who want to connect

88. What is included in the price of the class?
(A) Snacks
(B) Hot drinks
(C) Textbooks
(D) Free phones

Questions 89 to 91 refer to the following web page.

Forest Den Hotel Optional Tour

Take a night time walk in the snow through the forest. Led safely by our experienced guide. We will finish with hot chocolate by a fire. Everyone is welcome to join.

Every Sunday, Wednesday, and Friday

Meeting Place & Time: Hotel Lobby at 8 P.M.

Price: $10

Booking: Please make reservations at the front desk.

Check online for more details and don't forget to dress warmly.

89. What will happen at 8 P.M.?
(A) A guide will talk about the forest.
(B) A forest walk will start.
(C) Guests will sit by a fire.
(D) People will drink hot chocolate.

90. What is suggested about the walk?
(A) It will be cold.
(B) It is only for experienced hikers
(C) It is free.
(D) It will be in the morning.

91. How can people join the walk?
(A) By registering online
(B) By phoning the hotel
(C) By filling in a form in their room
(D) By making a reservation at reception

Questions 92 to 94 refer to the following information.

Walden Fishing Competition

The annual fishing competition will be held again this September. There will be the usual categories, of Professional, expert, and beginner. This year, we are pleased to announce a new category for the under 14s.

Cash prizes will be given for the professional category. Prizes of fishing gear will be given to the expert and beginner categories. The under 14s will win a trip on a fishing boat.

Other events on the day include fishing lessons with professionals, displays of new equipment, and workshops on how to prepare and cook river fish. Local restaurants will also set up food stalls.

For more information and to register online, please go to www.waldenboathouse.co.uk

92. What is suggested about this competition?

(A) It is a new.
(B) It is held every month.
(C) It is held every year.
(D) It is only for professional fishers.

92. What is the prize for the children's category?

(A) Money
(B) A ride on a boat
(C) A fishing boat
(D) Fishing rods

94. What is NOT included in the competition?

(A) Swim in the river
(B) Eat lunch
(C) Look at new finshing gears
(D) Learn how to cook

Questions 95 to 97 refer to the following article.

LIFE ONLINE

As smartphones have become widespread, there has been a change in how we work and play.

People are spending more time online chatting with friends and meeting new people. It is said that the average young adult person spends around 4 hours a day on phones, compared to only 30 minutes of watching TV. Young people no longer call each other. Most prefer to use chat apps. Some older people find this change difficult but many are learning how to use their phones.

Some say it is not a good way for people to spend too much time playing games. But others say smartphones have made anything possible. Many are choosing to study and learn new skills on their phones. Moreover, some people have set up new businesses only using their smartphones.

---

95. What is the article about?

(A) Online business
(B) The use of smartphones
(C) How to learn new skills
(D) Dating apps

96. How long do young people spend using their phone?

(A) Half an hour
(B) Four hours
(C) Half day
(D) All day

97. What does the article say about older people?

(A) They are learning how to use new technology.
(B) They don't watch TV.
(C) They are not interested in smartphones.
(D) They spend more time on their phones.

Questions 98 to 100 refer to the online chat conversation.

Jane: Hi. It was a great party last night! Sorry I had to leave early.

Sarah: No problem. It was really good to see you. Did you take many photos? My battery ran out. So I didn't get many.

Jane: Yes. I got some great ones with you blowing all the candles on your birthday cake. And some with the people form your office.

Sarah: Could you send them to me later?

Jane: Sure. Oh, and don't forget Mom and Dad's anniversary party next week!

98. What kind of party was it?
(A) An office party
(B) A birthday party
(C) A welcome party
(D) An anniversary party

99. What is suggested about Jane and Sarah?
(A) They work together.
(B) They are sisters.
(C) They live together.
(D) They are new friends.

100. What will Jane do next?
(A) E-mail photos
(B) Make a cake
(C) Recharge her phone battery
(D) Go to work

Stop!

This is the end of the Reading test. If you finish before time is called, you may go back to Reading Parts 1, 2, and 3 and check your work.

GOOD JOB! SCORE UP!

TOEIC Bridge Listening & Reading Sample Test （解答用紙）

Name ______________________________

LISTENING SECTION

No.	Answer	No.	Answer	No.	Answer	No.	Answer	No.	Answer
	A B C D		A B C D		A B C D		A B C D		A B C D
1	Ⓐ Ⓑ Ⓒ Ⓓ	11	Ⓐ Ⓑ Ⓒ Ⓓ	21	Ⓐ Ⓑ Ⓒ Ⓓ	31	Ⓐ Ⓑ Ⓒ Ⓓ	41	Ⓐ Ⓑ Ⓒ Ⓓ
2	Ⓐ Ⓑ Ⓒ Ⓓ	12	Ⓐ Ⓑ Ⓒ Ⓓ	22	Ⓐ Ⓑ Ⓒ Ⓓ	32	Ⓐ Ⓑ Ⓒ Ⓓ	42	Ⓐ Ⓑ Ⓒ Ⓓ
3	Ⓐ Ⓑ Ⓒ Ⓓ	13	Ⓐ Ⓑ Ⓒ Ⓓ	23	Ⓐ Ⓑ Ⓒ Ⓓ	33	Ⓐ Ⓑ Ⓒ Ⓓ	43	Ⓐ Ⓑ Ⓒ Ⓓ
4	Ⓐ Ⓑ Ⓒ Ⓓ	14	Ⓐ Ⓑ Ⓒ Ⓓ	24	Ⓐ Ⓑ Ⓒ Ⓓ	34	Ⓐ Ⓑ Ⓒ Ⓓ	44	Ⓐ Ⓑ Ⓒ Ⓓ
5	Ⓐ Ⓑ Ⓒ Ⓓ	15	Ⓐ Ⓑ Ⓒ Ⓓ	25	Ⓐ Ⓑ Ⓒ Ⓓ	35	Ⓐ Ⓑ Ⓒ Ⓓ	45	Ⓐ Ⓑ Ⓒ Ⓓ
6	Ⓐ Ⓑ Ⓒ Ⓓ	16	Ⓐ Ⓑ Ⓒ Ⓓ	26	Ⓐ Ⓑ Ⓒ Ⓓ	36	Ⓐ Ⓑ Ⓒ Ⓓ	46	Ⓐ Ⓑ Ⓒ Ⓓ
7	Ⓐ Ⓑ Ⓒ Ⓓ	17	Ⓐ Ⓑ Ⓒ Ⓓ	27	Ⓐ Ⓑ Ⓒ Ⓓ	37	Ⓐ Ⓑ Ⓒ Ⓓ	47	Ⓐ Ⓑ Ⓒ Ⓓ
8	Ⓐ Ⓑ Ⓒ Ⓓ	18	Ⓐ Ⓑ Ⓒ Ⓓ	28	Ⓐ Ⓑ Ⓒ Ⓓ	38	Ⓐ Ⓑ Ⓒ Ⓓ	48	Ⓐ Ⓑ Ⓒ Ⓓ
9	Ⓐ Ⓑ Ⓒ Ⓓ	19	Ⓐ Ⓑ Ⓒ Ⓓ	29	Ⓐ Ⓑ Ⓒ Ⓓ	39	Ⓐ Ⓑ Ⓒ Ⓓ	49	Ⓐ Ⓑ Ⓒ Ⓓ
10	Ⓐ Ⓑ Ⓒ Ⓓ	20	Ⓐ Ⓑ Ⓒ Ⓓ	30	Ⓐ Ⓑ Ⓒ Ⓓ	40	Ⓐ Ⓑ Ⓒ Ⓓ	50	Ⓐ Ⓑ Ⓒ Ⓓ

READING SECTION

No.	Answer	No.	Answer	No.	Answer	No.	Answer	No.	Answer
	A B C D		A B C D		A B C D		A B C D		A B C D
51	Ⓐ Ⓑ Ⓒ Ⓓ	61	Ⓐ Ⓑ Ⓒ Ⓓ	71	Ⓐ Ⓑ Ⓒ Ⓓ	81	Ⓐ Ⓑ Ⓒ Ⓓ	91	Ⓐ Ⓑ Ⓒ Ⓓ
52	Ⓐ Ⓑ Ⓒ Ⓓ	62	Ⓐ Ⓑ Ⓒ Ⓓ	72	Ⓐ Ⓑ Ⓒ Ⓓ	82	Ⓐ Ⓑ Ⓒ Ⓓ	92	Ⓐ Ⓑ Ⓒ Ⓓ
53	Ⓐ Ⓑ Ⓒ Ⓓ	63	Ⓐ Ⓑ Ⓒ Ⓓ	73	Ⓐ Ⓑ Ⓒ Ⓓ	83	Ⓐ Ⓑ Ⓒ Ⓓ	93	Ⓐ Ⓑ Ⓒ Ⓓ
54	Ⓐ Ⓑ Ⓒ Ⓓ	64	Ⓐ Ⓑ Ⓒ Ⓓ	74	Ⓐ Ⓑ Ⓒ Ⓓ	84	Ⓐ Ⓑ Ⓒ Ⓓ	94	Ⓐ Ⓑ Ⓒ Ⓓ
55	Ⓐ Ⓑ Ⓒ Ⓓ	65	Ⓐ Ⓑ Ⓒ Ⓓ	75	Ⓐ Ⓑ Ⓒ Ⓓ	85	Ⓐ Ⓑ Ⓒ Ⓓ	95	Ⓐ Ⓑ Ⓒ Ⓓ
56	Ⓐ Ⓑ Ⓒ Ⓓ	66	Ⓐ Ⓑ Ⓒ Ⓓ	76	Ⓐ Ⓑ Ⓒ Ⓓ	86	Ⓐ Ⓑ Ⓒ Ⓓ	96	Ⓐ Ⓑ Ⓒ Ⓓ
57	Ⓐ Ⓑ Ⓒ Ⓓ	67	Ⓐ Ⓑ Ⓒ Ⓓ	77	Ⓐ Ⓑ Ⓒ Ⓓ	87	Ⓐ Ⓑ Ⓒ Ⓓ	97	Ⓐ Ⓑ Ⓒ Ⓓ
58	Ⓐ Ⓑ Ⓒ Ⓓ	68	Ⓐ Ⓑ Ⓒ Ⓓ	78	Ⓐ Ⓑ Ⓒ Ⓓ	88	Ⓐ Ⓑ Ⓒ Ⓓ	98	Ⓐ Ⓑ Ⓒ Ⓓ
59	Ⓐ Ⓑ Ⓒ Ⓓ	69	Ⓐ Ⓑ Ⓒ Ⓓ	79	Ⓐ Ⓑ Ⓒ Ⓓ	89	Ⓐ Ⓑ Ⓒ Ⓓ	99	Ⓐ Ⓑ Ⓒ Ⓓ
60	Ⓐ Ⓑ Ⓒ Ⓓ	70	Ⓐ Ⓑ Ⓒ Ⓓ	80	Ⓐ Ⓑ Ⓒ Ⓓ	90	Ⓐ Ⓑ Ⓒ Ⓓ	100	Ⓐ Ⓑ Ⓒ Ⓓ

Companion to TOEIC Bridge® L&R Tests

Companion to TOEIC Bridge® L&R Tests　[B-925]
大学生のための TOEIC Bridge® L&R Tests 演習

1 刷　2021 年 2 月 16 日
2 刷　2022 年 3 月 30 日

著　者　Esther WAER　エスタ・ウェア
内田　雅克　UCHIDA Masakatsu
亀山　博之　KAMEYAMA Hiroyuki

発行者　南雲　一範　Kazunori Nagumo
発行所　株式会社　南雲堂
〒162-0801　東京都新宿区山吹町361
NAN’UN-DO Co., Ltd.
361 Yamabuki-cho, Shinjuku-ku, Tokyo 162-0801, Japan
振替口座 : 00160-0-46863
TEL:　03-3268-2311（営業部：学校関係）
03-3268-2384（営業部：書店関係）
03-3268-2387（編集部）
FAX:　03-3269-2486
編集者　加藤　敦

組　版　中西　史子

装　丁　奥定　泰之

イラスト　菊池　ひかり

検　印　省　略

コード　ISBN978-4-523-17925-2　C0082

Printed in Japan

E-mail : nanundo@post.email.ne.jp
URL : https://www.nanun-do.co.jp/